Contents

Part 1 Learning to Ride

Many people still think you have to be rich and live in the country to be able to ride. It's simply no longer the case. An estimated two million children and adults ride regularly in Britain, and the numbers are growing. Many of these people, particularly newcomers to the sport, do not own their own horses. They use the services of the many excellent riding schools which are often situated near towns and cities. If, after a while, you decide you want to ride your own horse, you can go ahead with some experience, knowing the likely pitfalls and costs.

This book will be particularly useful to those of you who do not have a 'horsey' background, and should help break down the feelings of apprehension that many people feel the first time they walk into a

The Pocket Guide to
RIDING

Jan Burgess

Bell & Hyman

The Pocket Guide to Riding
was designed and edited by
Holland & Clark Limited, London

Designer
Julian Holland

Editors
Philip Clark
Christine McMullen

Artist
Nicolas Hall

Photo Credits
ZEFA pages 6/7; Peter Roberts pages 14/15;
Mike Roberts pages 27, 39, 63, 75, 86/87;
Findlay Davidson pages 70/71, 72/73, 78/79;
Bob Langrish page 89.

Published by Bell & Hyman
Denmark House, 37/39 Queen Elizabeth Street,
London SE1 2QB

British Library Cataloguing in Publication Data
Burgess, Jan
   The pocket guide to riding.
   1. Horsemanship
   I. Title
   798.2'3   SF309

ISBN 0-7135-2512-6

Phototypeset in Great Britain by
Tradespools Limited, Frome, Somerset

Printed and bound in Great Britain by
Purnell & Sons Limited, Paulton

busy stable yard for a ride.

Part 1 concentrates on the process of learning to ride and will enable you to get the most out of your early lessons. The willing cooperation that takes place between horse and rider makes riding unique and there is nothing to beat the exhilaration and sense of achievement you will feel as you start to master the art.

Part 2 covers the main equestrian sports. A major reason for the growing popularity of riding is that television has brought showjumping and horse trials into the homes of millions. So even if you do not aspire to becoming a leading three-day-event rider, knowing more about the rules and organisation of the sport will help you enjoy watching the world's international riding events .

Glossary of Riding Terms

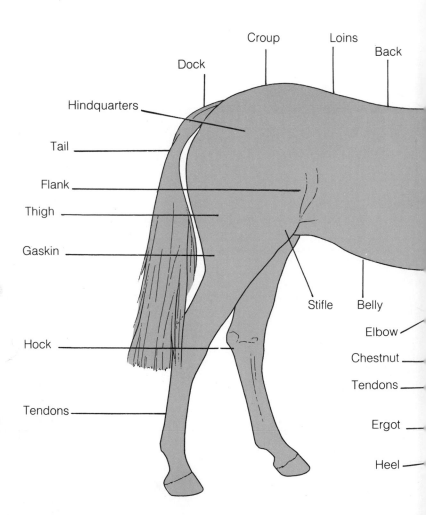

Croup

Loins

Back

Dock

Hindquarters

Tail

Flank

Thigh

Gaskin

Stifle

Belly

Elbow

Chestnut

Tendons

Hock

Ergot

Tendons

Heel

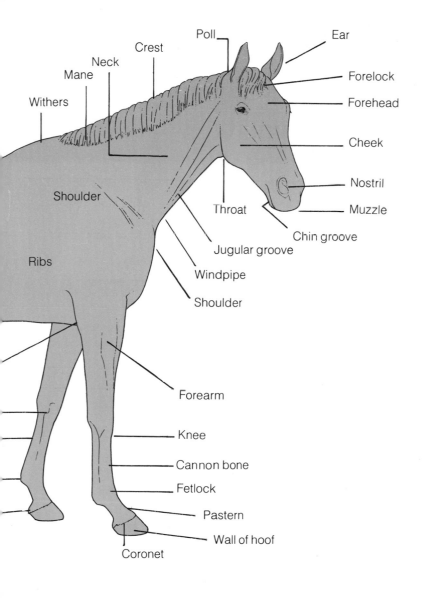

Poll

Ear

Crest

Neck

Forelock

Mane

Forehead

Withers

Cheek

Nostril

Shoulder

Muzzle

Throat

Ribs

Chin groove

Jugular groove

Windpipe

Shoulder

Forearm

Knee

Cannon bone

Fetlock

Pastern

Wall of hoof

Coronet

THE SADDLE

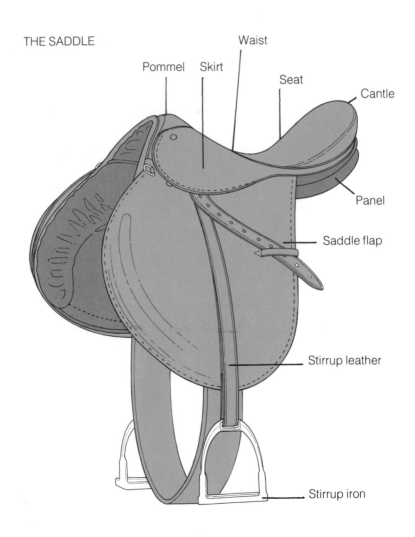

Pommel

Skirt

Waist

Seat

Cantle

Panel

Saddle flap

Stirrup leather

Stirrup iron

Aids The means by which the rider communicates with his or her horse.
Bit Device attached to the bridle and fitted in the horse's mouth so that the rider has control.
Break in To accustom the horse to being handled and ridden.
Cantle The back of the saddle.
Cast (a shoe) One that is lost;
(a horse) One that cannot rise from the ground, usually because it is trapped against a wall in its box.
Cavaletti Heavy wooden poles with cross pieces on either end, so that the height from the ground can be varied between 15–30 cm (6–12 in).
Cavesson noseband Particular type of noseband which fits round the horse's nose, above the level of the bit and inside the cheekpieces of the bridle.
Change of rein When a horse and rider on a circle change direction from anti-clockwise to clockwise and vice versa.
Clench The end of the shoeing nail which comes through the hoof.
Collection A horse is said to be collected when its natural outline is shortened, its centre of gravity raised and its hindquarters show increased impulsion.
Colt Ungelded male horse up to and including its third year.
Combination jump A show jump which consists of two or more parts. The distances between the parts are carefully planned by the course-builder to allow one or two strides, or a bounce in and out.
Conformation The physical build of a horse or pony.
Contact The rider must have contact between his hand and the horse's mouth. This is maintained via the reins.
Coronet The part of the horse's hoof from which the horny wall grows.
Diagonal A line from one corner diagonally to another.
Double bridle The bridle is double because it has two bits, a snaffle and a curb, and consequently two cheekpieces and two reins.
Filly Young, female horse up to and including its third year.
Foal A young horse up to a year old (when it becomes a yearling).
Forehand That part of the horse which is in front of the rider – the head and neck, shoulders, withers, chest and forelegs.
Forelock The part of the mane which comes forward over the horse's face.
Fullered This is a shoeing term which describes the deep groove made along the underside of the shoe to help prevent slipping.
Gait The pace of the horse – the walk, trot, canter and gallop.
Gaskin That part of the horse's hind leg above the hock and below the stifle.
Gelding Castrated male horse.
Girth Strap round the horse's belly which keeps the saddle in place. Also the measurement round the deepest part of the horse's body behind the withers.
Girth gall A sore caused by friction in the girth area. Caused by an ill-fitting or badly maintained girth, dirt trapped between the girth and the skin, or because the horse is unfit or overworked.
Good hands A rider is said to have good hands when he needs to use

the minimum of hand aids to control the horse. In other words, his hands are sensitive and quick to respond.

Ground line A clear indication of where the ground is at the foot of a jump, for example, a pole on the ground. A clear ground line helps the horse to estimate the correct take-off position and height to jump.

Hacking Riding out for pleasure as opposed to sport or competition.

Halter A simple rope arrangement with built-in lead rope, used instead of a headcollar.

Hand A measurement of 10 cm (4 in) used to describe the height of a horse. This is taken as the measurement from the top of the withers to the ground.

MEASURING
A HORSE

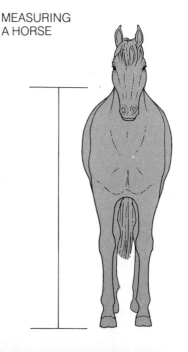

Headcollar A headpiece used for controlling the horse when it is not being ridden.

Impulsion The feeling of forward movement which dressage judges in particular, look for when marking a dressage test. It is built up by the rider's body, legs and seat and controlled by the reins.

Independent seat This is what all riders aim to achieve as quickly as possible. The rider is in balance with the horse, and able to use arms, legs, body and seat independently of each other.

Left rein/right rein When riding on the left rein, the horse describes a left-handed circle, and vice versa.

Leg-up A method of assisted mounting. The assistant stands close to the horse's near side, bends down and holds the rider's bent left knee and calf. At a pre-arranged signal, the assistant lifts the rider, thus giving him an extra boost up.

Livery stable A stable where privately owned horses are looked after for their owners in return for agreed charges.

Lunging A long rein is attached to the bridle or headcollar, and the horse is driven in a circle round the trainer.

Mare Female horse, as of its fourth birthday.

Martingale A device used to prevent a horse raising its head above the angle of control. A **running martingale** is attached at one end between the horse's legs to the girth, and at the other, divided in two, to each rein. A **standing martingale** is attached at one end to the girth and at the other to a cavesson noseband.

Mounting block A low platform upon which the rider stands when mounting.

Napping When a horse veers away from the direction in which the rider wants to go. An untrained horse will frequently nap towards other horses, an open gate etc.

Near side The horse's left side.

Numnah A shaped pad of fabric or sheepskin which fits under the saddle.

Off side The horse's right side.

Poll The top of the horse's head between the ears.

Pommel The front of the saddle.

Quarters The area behind the saddle down to the gaskin.

Rearing When a horse stands on its hind legs.

Rein back To make the horse step back.

Resistance When the horse disobeys the rider's aids. In competitions, it is used more particularly to mean refusing to go forward or rearing, and can earn penalties.

Saddle sores Friction or pressure sores in the saddle area, caused by an ill-fitting or badly maintained saddle, or occasionally by a bad rider, or because the horse is unfit or overworked.

Safety stirrups The outside edge of the stirrup iron is replaced by a strong elastic band. The idea being that the elastic band snaps if the rider falls, so that it is impossible to trap a foot in the stirrups. Unfortunately, the bands sometimes snap or get lost at the wrong moment!

Snaffle The simplest and most common type of bit, normally used by novice riders. **Snaffle bridle** A bridle fitted with a snaffle bit.

Stallion Male horse, over four years old, capable of siring young.

Strap A leather strap fitted round the horse's neck and attached to the saddle. A useful safety aid for beginners.

Tack The equipment put on a horse when it is being ridden to control if and make it safer

Thoroughbred This is a particular breed of horse. (The term 'purebred' is used to describe a horse of unmixed breeding.)

Throatlash Part of the bridle attached to the headpiece which passes under the horse's throat.

Track The course which a competitor is expected to follow in a showjumping event.

Transition A change from one pace to another.

Turned out A term used to describe keeping a horse in a field as opposed to a stable. It also describes the way a horse and rider look or have been prepared for an event.

Withers The part of the horse in front of the saddle and behind the neck.

Choosing a Riding School

Most people who learn to ride do not own their own horse. They start by going to a local riding school for lessons on hired animals. Learning this way has many advantages. A riding school can provide a choice of mounts, so you will be put on an animal suited to your build and experience. It is no use putting a beginner on an excitable thoroughbred, for example. Also, by learning with an instructor, you will not pick up

bad habits since any problems can be put right before they become established. As your experience broadens, you will have the opportunity to ride a wide variety of horses, and in the long run this is a tremendous practical advantage – each horse is different and techniques that work for one may have no effect at all on another mount.

Finally, as I hope you will find out, learning in a group is fun and the elements of competition and companionship grow as you progress.

By law, riding schools must be inspected regularly and licensed by the local authority. At the very least, such riding establishments will be properly insured. However, the standards laid down by the licensing authorities vary in different parts of the country. You are safer to look for an establishment which has been further 'approved' by one or more of the professional bodies which cater for the interests of riders. The British Horse Society, the Association of British Riding Schools and the Ponies of Britain Club all run their own inspection and approval schemes, and can provide lists of places to ride in your area (see pages 90–91 for addresses).

Some of the larger schools also take on students training to teach riding or to work as professional grooms. You will generally find that these schools are run by well-qualified staff and offer better than average training facilities, so it is worth looking out for them.

Whatever you do, check that the riding school you have chosen is licensed. Cowboy establishments do sometimes crop up, unnoticed by the local authority.

If you telephone to book your first lesson, the person you speak to should enquire about your height, weight and what experience you have had. It is better still to go to the riding school and ask to speak to the proprietor. You can learn a good deal about the place by looking around and talking. The proprietor should be able to tell you something about the teaching methods used, the sizes of groups taught and the kind of riding you will be able to do as you progress, whether that is hacking out in pleasant surroundings, show-jumping, cross-country, dressage or whatever.

Adults should make sure they will be taught with other adults since the

TYPICAL RIDING
SCHOOL LAYOUT

techniques for teaching novice adults and children are quite different.

The horses, of course, should look clean and well fed, but do not worry if the place is a little untidy. In a busy yard it is difficult to keep things spick and span all the time, when the daily routine of feeding, grooming and exercise has to fit in with the requirements of individual clients.

Below: An enclosed area where early lessons can take place is essential. This will give confidence to a novice rider as the horse cannot go very far on its own without being stopped by the surrounding barrier. The enclosure may be a complete indoor school or simply a marked out and fenced off schooling area in the open. Many establishments also have a lecture room.

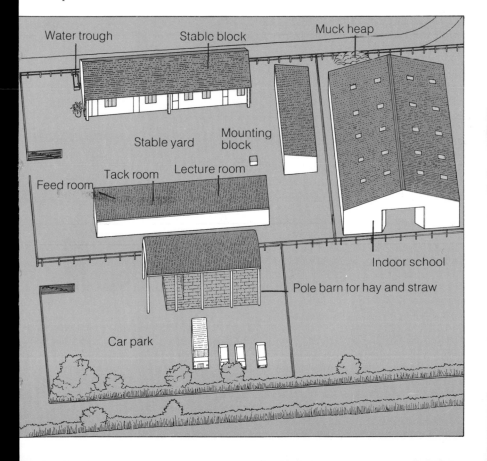

Water trough

Stable block

Muck heap

Stable yard

Mounting block

Tack room

Lecture room

Feed room

Indoor school

Pole barn for hay and straw

Car park

Riding Clothes

It is not really necessary to go out and buy a large quantity of expensive clothing before you start. For safety's sake, however, you should have a well-fitting hard hat with a strap under the chin. Some schools hire out hats, but these may be in poor condition and rarely fit properly, so it is worth investing in a hat if nothing else. It is illegal for children under sixteen to ride at a riding school without a hat.

The design of riding hats has been much criticised and is currently undergoing modification to make it safer. The traditional hat consists of a hard shell with a covering of velvet, usually black, and with an adjustable strap under the chin. You can also get harnesses which fit over the hat and under the chin. These should only be used on a hat with a flexible peak. Hats should be replaced every five years, and certainly if you have a fall in which you hit your head. The hat may not look damaged but once it has absorbed the impact of a fall, it will not go back to its original shape.

Also available is the crash cap which is always worn by racing jockeys and event riders. Crash caps rarely come off in a fall, and are made to a higher British Safety Standard. They are not worn widely by non-professional riders, though for no very good reason.

As well as a hat, you will need strong shoes or boots, with a slight but low heel to prevent the foot slipping through the stirrup. Wellingtons are not suitable as they may become caught in the stirrup. Loose-fitting trousers and a sweater or close-fitting anorak are all you need for your first few lessons.

Once you are 'hooked' on riding, there is a wide range of gear to choose from. Briefly, long rubber riding boots are practical and protect the legs from being pinched by the stirrup leathers.

Multi-stretch nylon jodhpurs in a variety of colours are comfortable and practical and are machine washable. You will find a close-fitting waterproof jacket useful. Avoid flapping nylon anoraks in lurid colours as they can excite a nervous horse.

You may find it helpful to wear gloves. String ones are good and help prevent the reins sliding through your fingers. In wet weather leather gloves are too slippery, so avoid them, and try not to have gloves that are bulky and make handling difficult.

A tweed hacking jacket is worn, as the name suggests, for hacking out and exercising. On more formal occasions, for showjumping, showing or dressage competitions, for instance, a black or navy-blue jacket is preferred with cream jodhpurs, boots, shirt and tie, hat and gloves. Women usually wear a hair net. It is common sense to tie back long hair when you are riding.

Finally, a word about sticks and whips. The main use of the stick is to reinforce any signal you give the horse with your legs and seat. A stick is rarely used to punish a horse. In fact, in most cases it just serves as a useful reminder to the horse and will make your ride a more pleasant one.

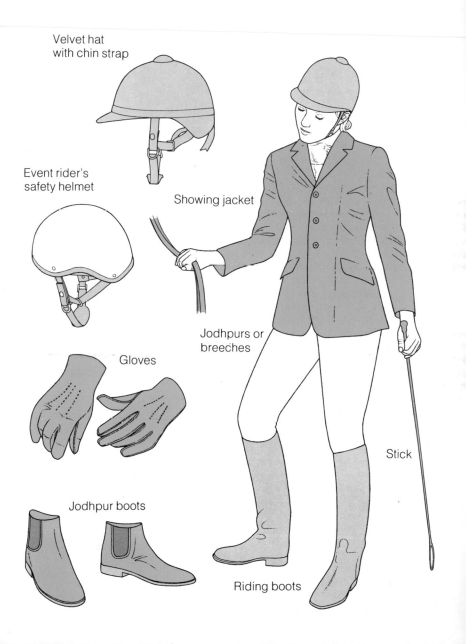

Velvet hat
with chin strap

Event rider's
safety helmet

Showing jacket

Gloves

Jodhpurs or
breeches

Stick

Jodhpur boots

Riding boots

The Tack

'Tack' is the name given to the leatherwork worn by the horse to give the rider a safer and more comfortable ride. At its simplest, this consists of a saddle and bridle but there are many different styles to serve the rider's various purposes, and the shape, size and temperament of individual horses.

The Saddle

The saddle is designed so that the mounted rider is 'in balance' with the horse. This means that the rider's weight is distributed over the horse's centre of gravity. For example, when a horse gallops, it stretches out its head and neck, and its centre of gravity moves forward. A racing saddle, therefore, is cut so that the jockey's weight is carried well forward over the horse's shoulders. For general purpose riding, saddle design is less extreme and the rider's weight is more centrally positioned. The saddle itself is designed to be comfortable and to help the rider to sit in the correct position.

It is vital that the saddle fits the horse correctly. Like an ill-fitting shoe, the wrong sized saddle can be

TYPES OF SADDLE

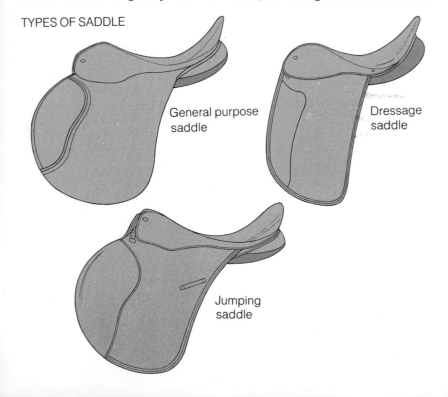

General purpose saddle

Dressage saddle

Jumping saddle

crippling. A numnah is sometimes used under the saddle. This is a saddle-shaped pad of fabric or sheepskin which makes the saddle comfortable for the horse. It should not be used to protect the horse from a badly fitting saddle.

The stirrups hang from adjustable leathers. The stirrup irons are usually made of steel, often with non-slip rubber treads. Safety stirrups are sometimes used for children.

The Bridle
Starting from the top, the bridle consists of the headpiece and throat-lash, browband, cheekpieces, noseband, bit and reins. The parts of the bridle are adjustable to some extent, but it must be the right size for the horse. Via the reins the rider brings about pressure on the horse's mouth, nose, poll and chin groove.

The novice usually begins to ride with a snaffle bridle but there are many different kinds.

During your first lessons, your horse will probably be tacked up for you. Later, a good school will show you how to tack up your own mount and how to check that the tack fits (see pages 56–59).

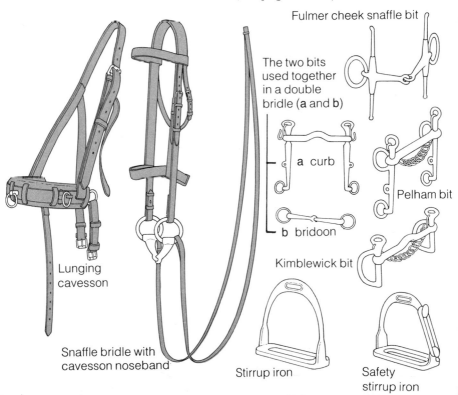

Fulmer cheek snaffle bit

The two bits used together in a double bridle (a and b)

a curb

b bridoon

Pelham bit

Kimblewick bit

Lunging cavesson

Snaffle bridle with cavesson noseband

Stirrup iron

Safety stirrup iron

Mounting

As a general rule, the horse gets used to being approached, tacked up, mounted and dismounted from the left or 'near' side. The commonest mistake in mounting is for the rider to haul himself up by pulling on the saddle and then to land heavily on the horse's back. Not surprisingly, the horse dislikes this and can also be injured. If the horse is large use a mounting block or ask for a 'leg-up'.

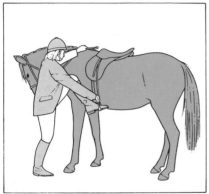

1. Hold the reins and stick in the left hand. Turn the stirrup clockwise, steady it with your right hand and slide in your left foot, toe down.

2. With two or three light hops, you are facing the horse, your left knee and calf pressed in close. Try not to prod the horse or it will walk forwards.

3. Spring up lightly, swinging the right leg carefully over the horse's back. Use your right hand to lean on the saddle, placing it on the pommel.

4. Land lightly in the saddle, find your off-side stirrup and gather up the reins. Don't let the horse move off until you are ready.

Dismounting

There are a number of ways of dismounting, but this method is the safest. Always take both feet out of the stirrups. Do not try to step down as this can be dangerous if the horse suddenly moves. It is unlikely that a horse will step on your foot unless, by accident, you kick it as you dismount. If this happens, push the horse's shoulder firmly away from you, saying 'over' at the same time and the horse should lift its hoof.

1. Make sure that the horse has come to a complete halt. Take both feet out of the stirrups and hold the reins and stick in your left hand.

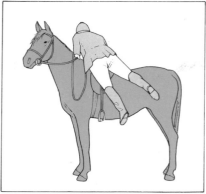

2. Lean forward slightly and swing your right leg over the horse's back. Use your right hand on the right side of the pommel to steady yourself.

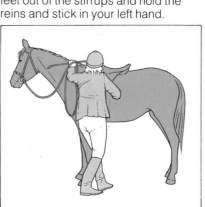

3. Slide gently down the horse's side, landing lightly on both feet, with knees slightly bent, close to the horse's side. Keep hold of the reins.

4. Take the reins over the horse's head, without letting go of them. If the horse has finished its work for the day prepare to remove its tack.

Adjusting the Tack

The Stirrups

At first, you may have to lengthen the near-side stirrup to make it easier to mount. With practice, however, you should be able to set the leather at roughly the right riding length before mounting. To do this, put your left hand at the top of the stirrup leather. Hold the stirrup iron in your right hand and it should reach your left armpit when your arm is stretched out straight.

Once mounted, take both feet out of the stirrups. As a rough guide the stirrup tread should be level with your ankle bone. The important thing is to feel comfortable and secure, so you may wish to adjust the leathers by a hole or two. As your experience grows, you will probably need to adjust the length.

The Girth

Before mounting, always check that the girth is tight. There is nothing more embarrassing than finding yourself sliding round under the horse's belly when the saddle slips. You should just be able to slide your fingers between the girth and the horse's side. After you have been out riding for about ten minutes, you should always re-check the girth. You may need to tighten it up by a further hole or two – a loose girth can be dangerous.

Below: Once the saddle is in position and the girth has been tightened, pulling out the horse's forelegs smooths out the skin under the girth and helps prevent girth galls. Do not let go of the reins while you do this.

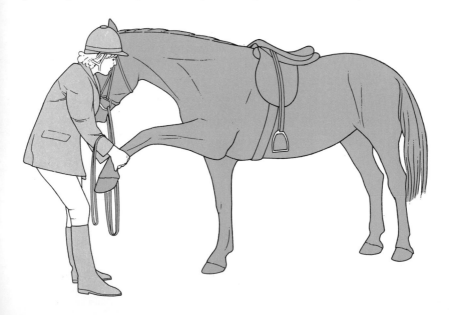

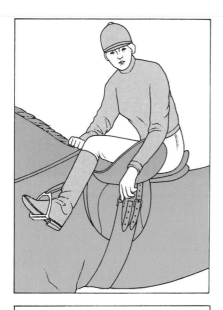

Tightening the Girth
With your foot in the stirrup, slide your leg forward. Reach under the saddle flap to find the girth buckles. Pull up the tab and, using your forefinger, guide the pin into the next hole. Remember to adjust both buckles.

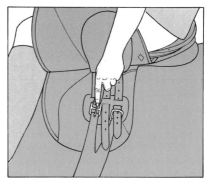

Adjusting the Stirrups
Keep your foot in the stirrup and take hold of the tab. Lengthen or shorten the leather and use your forefinger to guide the pin into the hole. Pull the inside leather down so that the buckle slides back up to the stirrup bar.

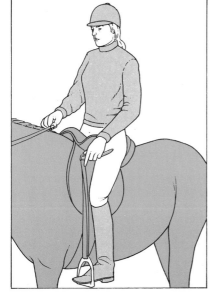

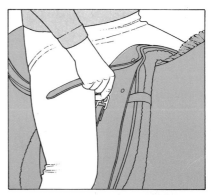

A Lesson on the Lunge

When a horse is on the lunge, it is controlled from the ground. One end of the lunge line is attached to the horse wearing a cavesson head collar over its bridle. The other end is in the hands of the handler or instructor. The instructor holds the lunge line like a rein. He can feel the horse's mouth almost as well as if he were riding himself, and can give instructions to halt and turn by pressure on the rein. This is backed up by voice commands, the whip, and even the way he stands. If he moves towards the horse's head and shoulder, this will tend to slow the horse. Moving behind the horse, towards its quarters, will tend to drive it forwards. Using these aids, the instructor drives the horse round him in a circle. He can control the speed and direction of the horse and this has obvious advantages for the rider.

Beginners

Some schools like to give beginners, especially adults, a short lesson or two on the lunge very early on. The advantages are that it builds up confidence, since the horse cannot possibly go anywhere except in a small circle. The rider does not have to think about controlling the horse, and can concentrate on sitting in a relaxed manner, and on trying to achieve a correct and secure riding position.

Finally, it helps to build up the right muscles – probably ones you didn't know you had! A lunge lesson is certainly much more strenuous than it looks, and 15 to 30 minutes at a time is probably enough.

Lunge Work

1. *Exercises performed by the rider.* These help to improve balance, develop muscle and counteract stiffness. They may include arm swinging, leg swinging, bending and twisting the torso. They may be performed with or without stirrups, in halt, walk and trot.

2. *Improving the riding position.* The instructor can devise exercises to correct individual faults and also show the rider how his own position affects the way the horse goes. For example, a heavy, bouncy rider can make a horse hollow its back and carry its head high in the air. A rider with his legs stuck too far forward cannot drive the horse forward effectively.

3. *Getting the feel of the different paces and the transitions between them.* Without having to worry about steering, the rider can really feel how the horse moves, and what each of its legs is doing at any moment. With practice, this becomes almost instinctive, and is essential for higher levels of dressage and jumping. In the early stages, it can be helpful to get the hang of, for instance, rising to the trot on the lunge, with the instructor at very close quarters to help.

Right: When a horse is being lunged for exercise or training purposes, it usually wears boots to protect its lower legs. A young horse, or a horse working round in a circle, is much more likely to strike itself than an older horse, or one going in a straight line. The metal shoes can injure the horse causing lameness.

The Correct Riding Position

Learning to ride takes quite a number of lessons. Some people sit on a horse and manage to look 'right' first time. For most of us, it takes time and practice. You cannot force your arms and legs into the right place, but there are things you can do which will help. Sit in the lowest part of the saddle, with a straight but not stiff back. Look up and ahead. Sit in the middle of the horse's back, not sliding to right or left (it helps to check that your stirrup leathers are of even length!).

Your arms should be relaxed, close to your sides, the elbows bent. By themselves, the stirrup leathers hang vertically. When you put your feet in the irons, you should not push the leathers forwards or backwards. Your legs should be relaxed and close to the horse's sides. Don't grip with your knees – this tends to force the thighs up the saddle, making you less secure. Let your weight sink down into your heels.

All this is more easily said than done. Don't concentrate so hard that you stiffen up! The horse is a living, moving creature, and you must be supple and able to move with it.

Below: In theory, a straight line could be drawn joining the rider's ear, shoulder, hip and heel. Another straight line goes from the elbow, through the wrist to the horse's mouth. The rider looks up and ahead. His weight sinks down through the knee, into the heel, so that the heel is slightly lower than the toe. Don't force the heel down.

The Wrong Position

This beginner is sitting in a typical wrong position. He is slumped in the saddle with the reins in loops, and his feet stuck forward. The rider looks uncomfortable and unprofessional but there are other problems too. With such a curved back, he has no way of influencing the way in which the horse goes. The looped reins mean lack of contact with the horse's head and the horse can do exactly what it wants. With his feet stuck forward, the rider is unlikely to fall over the horse's head, but it is also impossible for him to use his legs against the horse's sides to make it stop, start or turn.

Holding the Reins

If the reins are too long, they will fall into loops, and you will find it more difficult to maintain control. Also, you are more likely to pull on the horse's mouth accidentally, which is obviously to be avoided. If necessary, push your hands forward slightly to keep your reins the right length. The horse's head bobs back and forth as it moves, and your hands should also move gently to accommodate this action.

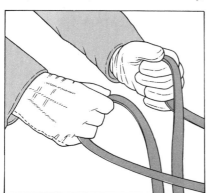

Left: The reins pass from the horse's mouth, between the rider's fourth and fifth fingers, and out between the first finger and thumb. The thumb anchors the rein to stop it slipping. As a starting-off point, your hand should be 10–15 cm (4–6 in) apart, and 10–15 cm (4–6 in) above the horse's withers.

It is important not to hang on to the reins to stop yourself falling back in the saddle. In the early days it is helpful to have a strap round the neck to hold on to when you feel insecure.

Communicating with the Horse

Natural Aids

The aids are the means by which you tell the horse what you want it to do. The natural aids are the seat, legs, hands and voice. Most beginners do not realise how important the seat is. But if you sit on your hands for a moment, move gently from side to side, and sit down hard, you should be able to feel how the pressure changes. If you sit forwards, rounding your shoulders, the pressure comes off your hands .

When you want to make the horse move forwards, the downwards pressure from your seat is the first signal it should feel. This is why your instructor will spend many hours trying to encourage a 'deep seat' – it makes you more secure in the saddle, and better able to communicate with the horse.

Pressure from the inside of the thigh or lower leg is used in conjunction with the seat. Put at its simplest, pressure from both legs will increase pace. Pressure from the right leg will make the horse move to the left. Pressure from the left leg will make it move to the right.

The horse's driving power comes from the back. This driving power, or 'impulsion' is controlled and directed by the hands on the reins. Soft squeezes on the reins are used in conjunction with the other aids to indicate to the horse that you want it to turn right or left, or slow down. A rider with harsh, unsympathetic hands will end up with an unhappy horse which is an unpleasant ride. 'Good hands' come once you can sit securely in the saddle and apply the aids without interfering with the horse's mouth, regardless of what the horse is doing at the time!

The voice also has its uses. A calm, quiet voice will calm a nervous animal. A firm 'No!' will often stop a horse which is about to do something silly. Making a 'clicking' or 'shss' noise to encourage the horse forward is an irritating habit for other riders around you, as their horses will get the same message.

Below: When you are mounted, your horse will let you know how it is feeling. Dismounted, you can learn about the horse, by interpreting its facial expressions.

FACIAL EXPRESSIONS

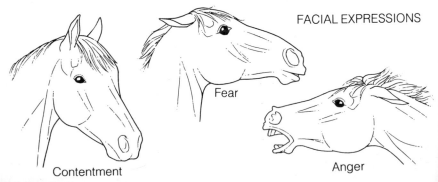

Fear

Contentment

Anger

Artificial Aids

This is the name given to certain items of equipment which may be used to back up the natural aids, chiefly whips, spurs and martingales. They are not nearly as important as the natural aids. In normal circumstances, a well trained, well balanced horse with a reasonably experienced rider does not need them at all. When an experienced rider does use spurs, it is always to refine an aid, never to punish a horse.

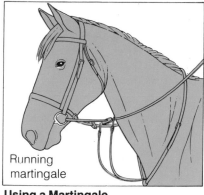

Running martingale

Standing martingale

Using a Martingale

Some horses, particularly excitable ones, may have a habit of throwing their heads up, which makes them very hard to control. A martingale can be used to prevent the horse from 'raising its head beyond the angle of control'

Using a Whip

A whip or stick can be useful, and it is a good idea to get used to carrying one. It has to be admitted that riding school horses sometimes get used to being ridden by beginners, and may take advantage of the situation! If your horse persistently ignores your aids, and you are sure you are giving them correctly, then of course, a sharp tap with the stick will remind it to take notice of you. Make sure you sometimes carry the stick in the right hand, sometimes in the left. You should learn to use the stick in both hands. This will be important once you start jumping.

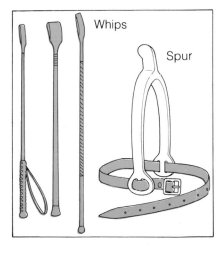

Whips

Spur

Riding at Walk

When you want to move from halt to walk, take up a contact on the reins (that is, make sure that there is a straight line between your fist and the horse's mouth, with no loops in the reins). Sit up straight in the saddle, push down slightly with your seat and squeeze gently with your lower legs.

It is important to think ahead about what you are going to do, before you do it. If you suddenly clap your legs against the horse's sides with no warning, you will not get a very good response from your horse. If you think first, you will automatically sit up and feel alert. The horse will sense that something is about to happen.

In walk, you will feel the horse's head and neck bobbing gently back and forth. Allow your hands to 'give' at each little bob. Do not try to push your hands back and forth or you will overdo it!

When you want to come back to halt, push down with your seat slightly, close your legs against the horse's side and keep your hands still, not allowing for the bob of the horse's head. Don't think about pulling back with the reins, but try to feel as if you are going forward into halt. Whenever you are riding, this feeling of forward impulsion is vital. Even when you are slowing down, you should feel as if you are controlling power and energy, not simply running out of it!

Changes from a slower pace to a faster one are called 'upward transitions', and from a faster to a slower, 'downward transitions'.

The walk is a four-time pace. That is, you can count a rhythm of 1-2-3-4 as each foot touches the ground. As you walk, try to feel the horse's legs under you and count out the rhythm. At first, you will probably count 1-2, 1-2. This is because you are only feeling the forelegs. Try to think about what is happening behind the saddle too.

In the free walk, the horse strides along with its head and neck stretched out. The rider has a long rein and a light contact. In practice, the medium walk is the one you will use most. The rider has a little more contact on the reins, the horse's head is raised a little, and it uses its hind legs more strongly to give a little more push. It is not just a question of making the horse walk faster! The collected walk is a more advanced pace in which the horse has to show some 'collection'.

There is nothing more irritating than a horse with a slouching, lazy walk. If you find this is happening to you, there are a number of checks you can make which should improve matters.

Is there a good contact between your hands and the horse's mouth? Simply throwing the reins forward does not help. Are you sitting on your whole seat, not leaning forward? Are you, in fact, using your seat as an aid? Are you keeping your legs close to the horse's sides and squeezing firmly, if necessary?

Sometimes you will see small children belabouring their ponies' sides with legs and heels in a vain attempt to produce faster forward motion. There may be many reasons for the lack of response, but certainly, repeated thumping is not the answer – it simply deadens the ponies' sensitivity to *any* aids.

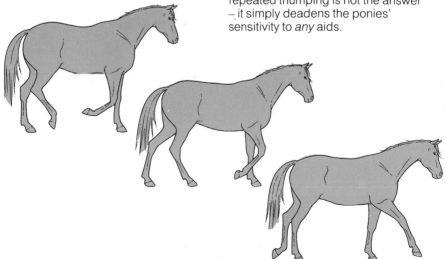

Riding at Trot

When you want to go from walk to trot, shorten your reins a little, push down with your seat and squeeze with your legs. The trot is a much bouncier pace than the walk and, at first, you will feel uncomfortable and out of synchronisation with the horse – which you probably are! There are two ways to cope with the bounce – by sitting in the saddle, or by rising and sitting alternately at each trotting step.

In theory, it should be easier to learn the sitting trot first. All you have to do is relax your lower back and hips, and 'go' with the movement of the horse. The first time a beginner experiences the trot and finds that he is bouncing in the saddle, he tends to tense up. The more he tenses, the more he bounces and the worse he feels. Relax! Feel as though your back is absorbing the horse's movement.

In rising trot, you cope with the bounce by allowing it to lift your seat out of the saddle at each step. Count 1-2, 1-2 with the beat of the forelegs, and try to feel that you are rising every time you count 2. Don't try to push up – the horse will do it for you.

To come back from trot to walk, sit in the saddle, close your legs against the horse's sides, and close your hands on the reins. Feel the rhythm change into the slower four-time of the walk. The trot is a knack, like riding a bicycle. Once you can do it, you never forget it.

The trot is a two-time pace. That is, you can count 1-2, 1-2 as the legs touch the ground. If you watch a horse trotting, you will see that its legs move in diagonal pairs. The off-hind and the near-fore touch the ground together, then the near-hind and the off-fore. In between, there is a period of suspension when all four legs are off the ground. This is the bounce that makes the trot seem so awkward for beginners.

Once you have got the hang of both sitting and rising to the trot, it is time to think about diagonals. As you trot, look for a moment at the horse's shoulders. You should be able to see each shoulder moving forward and back in turn. Then try to feel what each shoulder is doing without

looking. When you are riding in trot on a circle, you should ride on the outside diagonal. This means that as the outside foreleg touches the ground, you should be sitting (the foreleg is on the ground when the shoulder is coming back towards you).

To change the diagonal, you simply sit for one extra beat. When out for a ride, make a habit of checking your diagonal and changing it from time to time. It is surprising how one diagonal or another is more comfortable on a particular horse. You may find that you are constantly thrown on to a particular diagonal, and if you allow this to happen, the horse can become 'one-sided'.

The horse's head is steadier in trot than walk. As you sit and rise in the saddle, your elbow joints must open and close slightly, so that your hands can remain still and level.

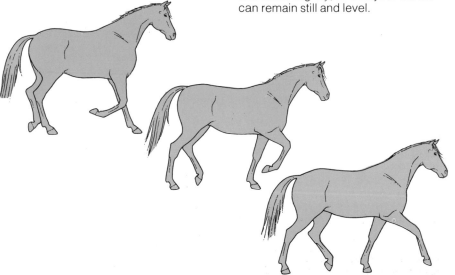

Improving Balance

In the old days, novice riders used to be taught to 'grip with your knees!' This was thought to be the best way to stay on. I remember riding round the school, with pennies or pieces of straw between my knees and the saddle, trying not to drop them.

Now, it is generally recognised that a deep, independent seat and balance are the best ways to be secure in the saddle. In fact, if you try to grip with your knees, you will find that it pushes the lower legs away from the horse's sides. You cannot give the aids effectively and you will be pushed up and out of the saddle. 'Gripping up', as this is called, is a common mistake.

Instead, let your thighs and knees relax and slide down the saddle flaps. Feel your weight sink down into your heels.

Exercises are a great help in developing good balance and a deep seat. Riding without stirrups is strenuous at first, but it really makes you rely on balance to stay firmly in the saddle. You cannot use the stirrups to take your weight and if you relax, it helps to eliminate gripping up (but it is no good if you hang on with your knees for grim death!)

While riding without stirrups, try moving both legs back from the hips. Feel how this opens up the angle of the hip, and helps move your thighs down the saddle. If you feel insecure without your stirrups at first, take both reins in one hand. (This should be the outside hand if you are riding in a circle in the school.) Hold the strap, mane or pommel with the other hand. Avoid using the reins to keep your balance.

1. Exercises like these should obviously be done only on quiet horses which are used to riders doing unusual things on their backs! Reaching forward to touch the ears increases mobility and confidence.

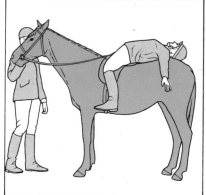

2. Only do this if you are fairly athletic and have strong stomach muscles. In any exercise, avoid dropping the reins. The horse may decide to walk off, and could tread on the reins and break them.

3. Swinging the legs alternately as though marching loosens up the hips. Try it in halt and walk. Move the whole leg. Avoid kicking the horse in the ribs or you may find yourself in a faster pace than you planned.

4. Sit straight in the saddle. Take the reins in one hand and reach up in the air with the other. Now bend down to touch the toe on the same side. Reach up again and, with the same hand, bend to reach the opposite toe.

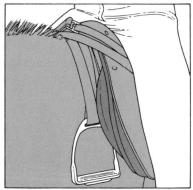

1. Riding without stirrups is a very useful exercise. The stirrups are crossed over in front of the pommel to prevent them banging about against the horse's sides.

2. When you are riding without stirrups, the buckles can be uncomfortable. Slide them down well clear of the stirrup bars before you cross them.

Beginner's Problems

A good riding school will teach you to ride on horses that know their jobs. This implies that they have been properly broken in, well looked after and have not developed any awkward habits. This kind of horse has been trained to respond to the aids, regardless of who is on its back. If your horse does not seem to be responding, check what you are doing before you blame your mount. Perhaps your aids are not clear enough. It does take time and practice to give the aids in a co-ordinated way, and to develop the necessary strength in your back and legs.

1. *My horse walks off when I try to mount.*
Before mounting, take the reins in your left hand near the horse's withers. Make sure there is a contact between your hands and the horse's mouth. The off-side rein should be slightly shorter. Avoid kicking the horse as you swing your leg over. If the horse does move forward, bring it back to halt straight away, before you move off.

2. *I keep losing my stirrups.*
Perhaps your stirrups are too long. More likely, you are 'gripping up'. Try to relax your thighs and knees. In trot, try standing in the stirrups for a few paces and feel your weight sinking into your heels. It is also a good idea to practise taking your feet out of the stirrups and then finding them again with your feet without looking down.

3. *I can't get my horse to go.*
Some riding schools put beginners on very quiet horses for obvious reasons. The trouble is that a quiet horse may also be unresponsive to the aids, and this is just as bad for a beginner as an over-excitable horse. However, you might be surprised at how the same horse is transformed when your instructor rides it. The reason is that riding school horses in particular get to know who is riding them, and can take advantage of an inexperienced rider. The answer is to be more positive. If your horse insists on standing by a hedge nibbling at a tasty shoot, don't just sit there and let it! Turn its head gently but firmly away, take up a good contact on the reins, and use your back, seat and legs to push the horse forward.

4. *I cannot do the sitting trot.*
It takes time for some people to feel really relaxed on a horse. For them it is often easier to learn the rising trot first. Once you feel confident, try the sitting trot again. Count the rhythm of the forelegs and swing your hips forwards at each beat. It may help to round your lower back a little so your hips and seat are pushed forward slightly. The movement of your seat and back absorb the bounce.

5. *I feel nervous of falling off.*
The first time they sit on a horse, most people are surprised at how far off the ground they feel. It looks a long way to fall! In fact, novice riders very rarely fall, because their horses are reliable and their work is well supervised.

Right: One of the pleasures of learning to ride is that you can often reach parts of the countryside which are quite inaccessible by other means.

Being Around Horses

Like many sports, there is an element of danger attached to riding, but there is much you can do to minimise the risk. After a while, as you get used to being around horses, riding them and handling them, you will develop a kind of 'horse sense'. You will get to know, for example, which horses tend to dislike company in their stables, and which ones to avoid while they are having a feed. In the meantime, there are certain things to bear in mind.

The horse is a domesticated animal, but deep down it still retains the instincts of a wild animal. The wild horse had to be constantly on the lookout for danger. Its only defence against attack was to run or, if cornered, to fight with hooves and teeth. Generations of domestication have overlaid these instincts, but horses are still easily startled and will run or kick out if frightened or roughly treated.

So, always approach a horse where it can see you i.e. towards its shoulder. Speak to it first, then give it a pat, and only then go ahead and put on its headcollar, or whatever. Try to avoid walking close behind a horse. Most horses do not kick, but it is as well not to put yourself in a position where you might be a target.

Be particularly careful when handling the horse's head. Many horses are sensitive about having a bridle put on, and need care and patience.

Avoid giving titbits to horses, especially in a riding school. A horse will quickly learn to expect food, and may start to snap at hands and pockets. At any rate, never feed anything to a horse without consulting its owner. Stabled horses have extraordinarily delicate digestive systems, which are easily upset!

Safety when Mounted

Before you mount, make a habit of running your eye over the horse's tack. Although in theory this is the responsibility of the riding school, it is only sensible for your own sake to check it. There should be no broken stitching or cracked leather. The tack should be correctly assembled

Leading the Horse in Hand
Once dismounted, take the reins over the horse's head. Loop them over your arm while you loosen the girths. Run the stirrup irons up the leathers. Tuck the leathers down through the irons to prevent them slipping down. Stand at the horse's nearside shoulder, holding the reins about 23 cm (9 in) from its mouth, with knuckles uppermost. Ask the horse firmly to 'walk on', and walk forward yourself. If the horse is slow to respond, have a whip in your left hand and give a smart tap behind the girth. It should not be necessary to drag the horse after you!

and fitted. Check the girth at this point and again after you have been riding for ten minutes or so.

If you are mounting in a busy yard, try to find a space away from other horses. It is sensible to avoid being caught midway between ground and saddle while your horse tries to bite or kick another one! When riding, avoid getting too close to other horses. Standing in a group with either noses or tails together invites snapping and kicking.

During a lesson, your instructor will probably ask you to keep a certain distance away from the next horse. One horse's length is about right in normal circumstances.

Never drop the reins completely, and never try to put on or take off a jacket while mounted, however confident you are that your horse is quiet and predictable.

Horses respond to kind but firm treatment. If you can generate a sense of quiet confidence, whatever you might be feeling, all the better. An over-excited horse will respond to a firm voice and handling, where panic in the rider will only make matters worse.

If you are ever out on a ride in a group, and someone should fall, you should immediately halt and wait for instructions from whoever is accompanying you.

The most important single safety rule is to wear a hard hat. The number of experienced riders who ignore this rule is extraordinary. Statistics show that it is the riders who do not have protective headgear who come to harm. This is especially true of accidents which happen on the road or other hard surface. It is no use whatever wearing a hat which is not secured to your head. Use either an adjustable strap under the chin, or a separate harness over the hat with a chin cup. A hat without a strap can be easily dislodged in a fall.

The Canter

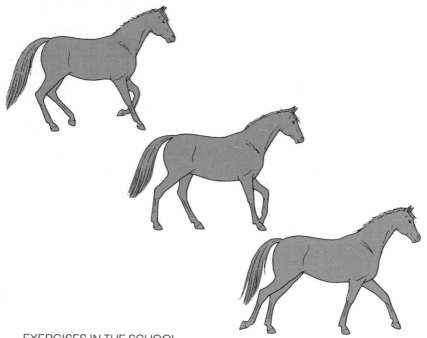

EXERCISES IN THE SCHOOL

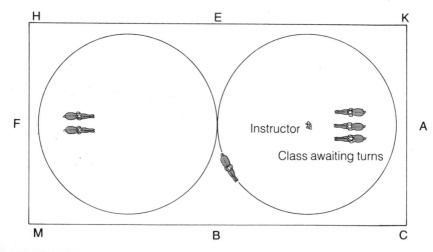

Before attempting the canter, you should feel secure in the trot. The canter is a surprisingly smooth and enjoyable pace once you get the hang of it. Your first attempts should be in the school. Later on, it helps if you can find a gentle uphill slope, since the horse will probably canter on easily, and slow down at the top. Try not to let yourself be thrown forward out of the saddle – you will only bounce uncomfortably. Sit in the saddle, relax your hips and let them swing forwards with each canter stride. If you find yourself bouncing, slow down to a trot and try again. The movement of your lower back, hips and seat must absorb the bounce in the canter stride, so don't stiffen up!

The canter is a three-time pace. If you watch a horse cantering, you will see that one of its forelegs is consistently thrown out further in front than the other. A horse is said to be cantering with a left leading leg, when the left leg swings forward furthest, and on the right lead, when the right leg is out in front. The sequence of leg movements in canter for a left lead is as follows: off-hind, followed by near-hind and off-fore together, followed by the leading near-fore.

Once you have got the basic feel of the canter, you should always decide which leg your horse is to strike off on when it goes into canter. If you don't, there is the likelihood that the horse will always choose to lead on the same leg, so becoming stiff and 'one-sided'. More important, it is dangerous to canter round a corner with the *outside* leg leading – your horse could easily trip or slip and fall.

Left: A useful cantering exercise is to ride a figure-of-eight. As you cross the middle of the school go from canter to trot and apply the aids for the opposite leading leg. To get the correct leading leg think of riding two 20 metre circles that touch.

The Gallop

The gallop is a four-time pace. The horse stretches out its neck and body as it accelerates, so that its centre of gravity moves forwards. There is a period of suspension when all four feet are off the ground. To stay in balance with the horse, the rider shortens the stirrups slightly, and takes weight off the horse's back, down through the thighs and knees, on to the ball of the foot. This moves the rider's weight forwards slightly.

Riding in a Group

The gallop should always be avoided when you are riding with a group. You may feel perfectly in control, but if you disappear over the horizon in a cloud of dust, it is very difficult for anyone else who does not want to go so fast to remain behind.

The gallop is a pace for very experienced riders only. The rider has to stay in balance with the horse, and this is not always easy at speed, should the horse swerve unexpectedly. If the rider does not stay in balance, he risks not only falling off, but also causing the horse to fall.

Having said this, many an unfortunate rider has found himself travelling a little faster in canter than he intended. The best way to avoid this happening is to nip it in the bud right at the beginning. As you feel the horse start to accelerate, immediately give slowing down aids. Otherwise, remember that it is no good just heaving on the reins. The horse is stronger than you, and will win any pulling battle. Give a firm squeeze on the reins and then release again. Repeat until the horse responds.

For the horse to travel at its fastest, your weight has to be poised forward, over its shoulder. Resist the temptation, therefore, to lean forward and hang on to the reins. You will only make matters worse! Sit back firmly in the saddle, keep your legs still and close to the horse's sides. Use your back and shoulder blades to reinforce the rein aids if necessary, and think calmly of trot.

If you are really out of control, the safest thing to do is to turn the horse on to a wide circle. This usually has a calming effect on an excited horse. Gradually, make the circle smaller and the horse will slow down.

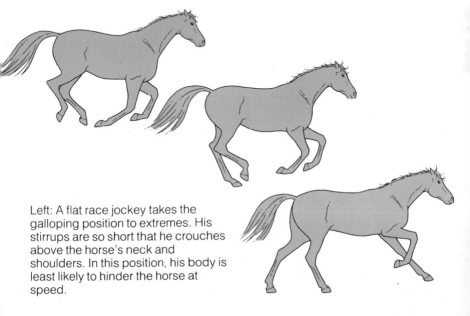

Left: A flat race jockey takes the galloping position to extremes. His stirrups are so short that he crouches above the horse's neck and shoulders. In this position, his body is least likely to hinder the horse at speed.

Riding in the School

The enclosed schooling area (or manège) may be indoors or outside. Part of it, at least, should be marked out as a dressage arena. When a group of riders are working independently in the school, there are a few rules of the road which help prevent bottlenecks and collisions.

1. Pass left shoulder to left shoulder.
2. The rider on the main track has right of way, so slow down or speed up to avoid other horses when joining the track.
3. Horses in the faster paces have right of way over slower ones, but do not be dogmatic about this!
4. When a group of riders is, for example, warming up for a lesson, it avoids confusion if the whole group rides first on the left rein (i.e. in an anti-clockwise direction), and then on the right rein (in a clockwise direction).

Turns

To make a turn, first check your position is correct, and steady the horse's pace. Use your outside leg firmly behind the girth to push the quarters into the turn. The inside leg should be on the girth. It acts as a pivot, round which the horse's body bends smoothly. The hands need do very little. The inside hand squeezes very gently, until the horse is looking in the direction of the turn – you should just be able to see the horse's eyelashes. Don't drop the outside rein into loops, maintain a steady contact. Make sure you do not lean into the turn, collapsing your inside hip, or the horse will 'fall in' too. Once the turn is complete, ride on, checking that your horse is 'straight'.

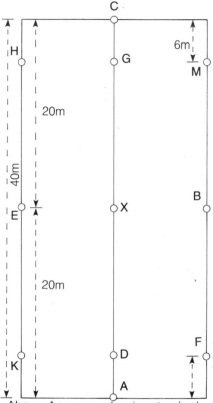

Above: A manege showing standard distances and markers.

Right: Riding school figures encourages you to be accurate and precise with your aids. For the horse they have the effect of gymnastic exercises.
1. A change of rein diagonally across the school, from K to M, or M to K.
2. 20 m circles .
3. Deep loops from the track to X and back again, starting at K, H, F or M.
4. Three equal loops down the school .

Exercises for riding in the manège

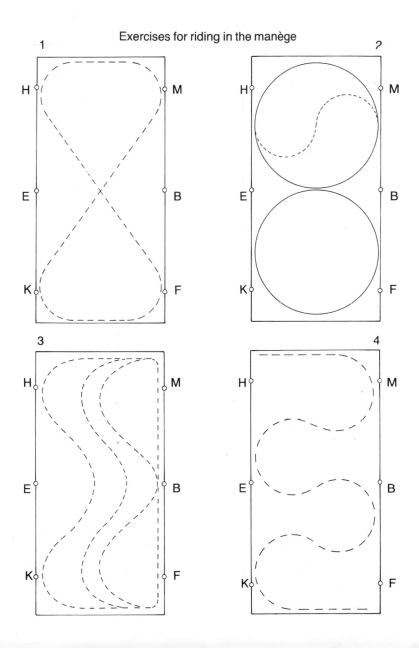

Lateral Movements

Going Straight
Making the horse 'go straight' is not as easy as it sounds. To be 'straight', the horse's hind legs should follow exactly in the tracks of the forelegs.

The horse's 'engine' is in its hind-quarters. When a horse is using its quarters energetically in walk, the hind feet overstep the prints of the forefeet by a good 15 cm (6 in) or so.

A horse should still be 'straight' when it is ridden round a corner. That is to say, its body should bend smoothly along its length from poll to tail, so that the hind feet still follow the tracks of the fore feet. What happens all too easily is that the horse turns stiffly, the quarters swinging out round the curve. Whenever you turn, make your aids deliberate and clear – inside leg on the girth acting as a pivot, outside leg behind the girth, activating the hind legs and pushing the quarters in, a slight bend of the horse's head in the direction of the curve, supported by the outside hand. Slight pressure on the inside seatbone helps, but do not overdo this and collapse your hip completely.

Work on Two Tracks
When the horse is going straight, it is said to be going on a single track. For more advanced dressage, for basic jumping and for quite simple manoeuvres, like opening and closing gates, it is helpful to be able to make the horse move sideways to some extent. Sideways movements, or lateral movements, involve work on two tracks. In other words, the horse's hind legs do not, and are not meant to follow the track of the forelegs. Before you can begin lateral movements, you must have a reasonably strong and independent seat, and be able to co-ordinate your aids effectively.

Leg Yielding
This is the simplest of the lateral movements, and it is the first to be taught to young horses and novice riders alike. As the name suggests, the horse yields to the leg, moving away from pressure from the rider.

In walk, initially, the horse moves sideways as well as forwards so that it advances diagonally. Its head is turned very slightly away from the direction in which it is going (in more advanced movements, the head is always turned towards the direction of progress).

To try leg yielding, make sure your horse is walking forwards freely and actively, and is paying attention to your aids. On the left rein, for example, turn down the centre line of the school (from A to C). To leg yield to the left, feel the right rein so that the horse's head is turned slightly to the right. Let your left hand come out and away from the horse's neck so that it can 'lead' the horse in the direction you want to go. Now close your legs, with the left leg on the girth, and the right leg a little behind the girth. Little nudges inwards with your right lower leg and foot may help. Feel that you are pushing the horse forwards and sideways from your right leg towards your left hand. Do not drop your contact on the reins, or the horse will just walk forwards faster.

Evasions

When you are learning to leg yield, it is important that the horse should know and understand the instructions you are endeavouring to give. However, lateral movements of any kind are more difficult for the horse than single-track work and you may find that response to your aids is slow or not very positive.

If the horse simply walks faster, use your hands sensitively to stop the horse escaping forwards. As soon as you do feel the horse obey by yielding, however slightly, reward it by 'giving' with the hands immediately. If the horse resists by slowing down, make it walk or trot forwards actively before trying again. Use your seat and legs more strongly next time to maintain forward impulsion.

Do not be too ambitious if you are both finding the exercise difficult.

Above: This horse and rider are leg yielding to the right. The movement is forwards as well as sideways, with the left legs coming across in advance of the right legs. As well as being useful in practical ways, leg yielding helps the horse become more flexible and better balanced. It gives the rider greater co-ordination, as well as the satisfaction of obtaining the co-operation of the horse in a relatively difficult manoeuvre.

After a few steps of leg yielding, ride straight forwards and give the horse a pat. You can try a few more steps next time round, until eventually you can go diagonally from the centre line to the far quarter markers, or even to E or B. You will usually find that this exercise is easier to carry out on one rein than another. Make sure you practise equally in both directions.

Halt and Rein Back

Halt

Most people manage to come to a stop reasonably successfully, but by now you should be thinking about what exactly you are trying to achieve when you halt. First of all, the horse should halt fair and square, the fore and hind legs in pairs, not splayed out all over the place. The horse should not throw its head up, or step sideways or backwards once it has come to a halt.

A good halt is easier to perform on a well trained horse, but you can play your part in helping any horse do its best. The aids to halt are the same as for a decrease in pace. Close your legs on the horse's sides and squeeze and release with your hands. Straighten your back a little at the same time. The leg aids in halt are often forgotten but are extremely important. They keep the horse going forward into halt, rather than drifting inattentively.

Rein Back

Make sure the horse is walking forwards with energy, and paying attention to your aids. Come to a good square halt. Pause momentarily. Then, close your legs round the horse as if asking for forwards movement. Instead of giving with your hands, resist gently. After three or four backward steps, ride firmly forwards to maintain impulsion.

The rein back is a two-time movement, in which the horse puts its feet down in diagonally opposite pairs. It should be practised on a horse that knows its job, because it is an extremely difficult movement to perform correctly.

Wrong Way
All too often, the rein back looks like this. The horse hollows its back, with its head in the air. The horse may not understand its rider's aids, or they may be applied too roughly.

Right Way
In a good rein back, the horse does not raise its head, but accepts the bit. It steps back cleanly and smoothly, and remains 'straight', with quarters swinging neither right nor left.

Turn on the Forehand

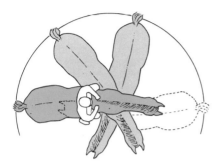

Turn on the Forehand
In a half turn on the forehand, the horse turns through 180° pivoting on one of its forelegs. In a right turn, the horse turns its body so that it ends up looking to the right. In a left turn the procedure is reversed.

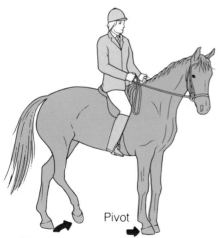

Above: In a correct right turn, the horse crosses its off hind leg over in front of the near hind. It pivots on the off fore, picking up and putting down the forelegs in the same place, but not moving forwards or back.

The turn on the forehand is just what it says. The horse moves in a circle, pivoting on its forehand. The front legs stay in the same spot, while the quarters move round in a quarter or half circle. It is technically a lateral movement and is useful because it gives you real control over the horse's quarters. You can swing the quarters away from traffic, for example, or move the horse round when you are trying to open a gate.

Start by trying a quarter turn. Make sure your horse is attentive and walking with energy. If you are in the school, it is usual to come off the track to the inside, making sure there is plenty of space around you. For a right turn on the forehand, have your stick in the right hand. Come to a good square halt. Bend the horse's head *slightly* to the right, maintaining your contact with the horse's mouth on your left rein, ready to stop it walking forwards if necessary. Close your legs with your right leg behind the girth, pushing the quarters over to the left. The left leg should be on the girth, ready to come into play more strongly should the horse try to step back or sideways. This is the leg which is often forgotten. Once you have completed a quarter turn, ride strongly forwards and give the horse a pat.

The first time you try this will probably be a disaster, since it is quite difficult to co-ordinate hands and legs, *and* respond to what the horse is doing. Watch your instructor again, be positive with your aids, but sensitive. Reward the horse by giving the rein as soon as you get the desired response.

Out for a Ride

You will have your first lessons in a contained area, such as an indoor school. There will quickly come a time when you will want to leave the security of the school and go out for a ride. After all, this is what most people learn to ride for! A group of eight or so riders is always accompanied by an experienced guide.

Do not become a passenger the moment you exit from the school gates. The horse will probably know its way better than you, and will happily slouch along behind the one in front if you let it. Put into practice what you have learned. Obviously, the group will go in the same general direction, but it is up to you to ride your horse, decide which path to take and the distance to keep between you and the other horses. Make your turns deliberately, change your diagonal in trot, choose which leading leg you want in canter, and you will get much more enjoyment and satisfaction.

You may find you are riding up and down some quite steep banks and slopes. This is excellent for improving your seat and balance.

Opening and Closing Gates

Approach the gate towards the latch end, so that you are standing parallel to it. If the gate opens towards you, pull it open. Now use the turn on the forehand to turn the horse round until you can ride forward and through the gate. Turn round and come back to close the gate behind you. If the gate opens away from you, walk gently forwards, and the horse will push it open with its chest.

Lean forward slightly when going uphill to help the horse. Sit upright when going downhill. In both cases, let the horse have a slightly longer rein than usual so that it can stretch out its head and neck to keep its balance and pick its way if the ground is uneven. However, do not drop all contact. Keep the pace steady, but be prepared to ride the horse forward if necessary. If you feel insecure, hold the mane or pommel.

It is tempting, at first, to ride along staring at the ground, looking for bumps and holes that your horse might trip over. If you ride positively, with a good contact on the reins, and your legs on the horse's sides it will look after its own feet. You would be better occupied looking ahead, planning your route.

When riding in the countryside, observe the usual rules of the country code. Be courteous, shut gates, stick to bridleways, do not trample on crops etc. In addition, for safety's sake do not get too far ahead or behind the rest of the group. If your guide opens a gate for you, file through and wait quietly while the gate is closed. If you continue on into the next field, the horse left behind will become increasingly impatient and may misbehave and buck in an attempt to catch up with the others.

Never increase your pace until the whole group is ready. In particular, when cantering, make sure you stay firmly in control to avoid starting a Grand National style stampede. Never canter round a blind corner – you may come across an old lady exercising her dog.

When riding downhill, sit firmly in the saddle, in an upright position. It is safest to ride straight down a steep slope. If the horse slips, its quarters will come directly under it and it is not likely to start a dangerous roll.

When riding up a long, steep hill, take your weight off the horse's back by leaning forward, so that it can use its quarters freely. A horse tends to rush quickly up a short slope so be prepared to keep the pace steady.

Riding on Roads

Riding on the roads is potentially more hazardous than riding in fields or on open land. Obviously, there is the danger of traffic, but also, in the case of a fall, you are landing on a hard surface, not yielding turf.

Safety on the Road
Unfortunately, the number of accidents involving riders is increasing, but there are some commonsense rules which minimise the risks.

The horses used for novice riders in riding schools should be absolutely reliable in traffic. However, sooner or later you may wish to ride less experienced horses, or find that your horse has come face to face with a double decker bus for the first time.

It is absolutely essential to wear a hard hat. This is vitally important when you are riding on hard surfaces. You should ride on the same side of the road as the traffic, i.e. on the left in Britain. Hold your whip in your right hand, i.e. between your horse and the traffic – the horse will naturally tend to move away from the whip and towards the side of the road.

Stick to walk or a steady trot when riding on tarmac. Road surfaces do not provide much grip for the horse's iron-shod foot, especially in rain or frost. The ungiving nature of the road surface also jars horses' legs, which can lead to strains and lameness.

Car drivers are not always used to horses, and tend to treat them as they would cyclists – getting very close to them at junctions and when overtaking. It is as well to be pre-pared for this, for a nervous rider transmits his feelings to his horse.

Occasionally a horse will baulk at an unfamiliar vehicle. Resist the temptation to turn the horse's head away from the road and into the hedge. This will only swing the quarters into the road, making you more vulnerable. If necessary, a few steps of the turn on the forehand will push the horse's quarters away from the 'obstacle', and give the horse a chance to have a good look at it. Better still, sit deep in the saddle with your legs in contact with the horse's sides, and ride firmly forwards. Be positive and look ahead where you want to go, not at the offending vehicle. If this does not avail, a more experienced horse and rider can help by riding just ahead of you to 'give a lead'.

The best preparation for riding in traffic is to take the British Horse Society Riding and Road Safety test.

GOLDEN RULES

DON'T forget to acknowledge courtesy from other road users – a wave or a smile helps improve public relations.

DON'T ride an inexperienced horse on busy roads.

DON'T ride faster than walk or trot.

DON'T ride on icy roads.

DON'T straggle across a road if

Above: Most horses regularly ridden on country roads get used to the sight of farm vehicles. Do not tense up yourself in anticipation of trouble, or you may cause a problem when none existed! Turn the horse's head very slightly so that it can take a good look at any traffic. Take up a proper contact on the reins, keep your legs close to the horse's sides, sit deep and ride firmly forwards. If the horse moves sideways towards the vehicle, be ready to use the leg nearest the traffic to push the horse back .

you are riding in a group. Keep together and walk briskly.

DON'T ride more than two abreast.

DON'T ride in the fog or failing light, if you can help it.

DON'T panic if your horse misbehaves. Ride it firmly forwards.

DO wear a hard hat.

DO take the British Horse Society Riding and Road Safety exam.

DO remember other road users. Make your intentions clear, and acknowledge their courtesy.

DO check your tack before starting out on your ride.

DO use reflective safety equipment, such as legbands and stirrup lamp, if you ever have to ride in failing light.

DO make sure your horse is used to traffic and has been taught 'road sense' before taking it on busy roads.

Preparing for a Ride

When you go for your first few riding lessons, you will be far too busy thinking about how to ride to worry about how the horse has been prepared for you. As you become more experienced, you may wish to get more involved with the 'background' work.

Assuming that the horse you are planning to ride is waiting for you in its stable, the first thing to do is gather up the equipment you need. Find the correct saddle, bridle and any other tack it usually wears. You will also need a headcollar, a dandy brush and a hoofpick. A dandy brush has stiff bristles, and is used for removing mud and dirt from the hair. If the horse has been clipped, or has a sensitive skin, you may need to use the softer-bristled body brush.

Leave your saddle and bridle outside the stable. Hang the bridle over the top half-door. Place the saddle so it sits upright on the front arch. If necessary, lean the cantle against the wall. To avoid damaging the leather, place the girth between the cantle and the wall for extra protection. Make sure you put the saddle down where it will not be kicked by other horses. Avoid putting it over the half-door as it is very likely to be knocked off and damaged.

As you go into the stable, speak to the horse to attract its attention, and remember to shut the door behind you. Approach the horse from the nearside, give it a pat, and put on the headcollar. Tie up the horse using a quick-release knot (see right).

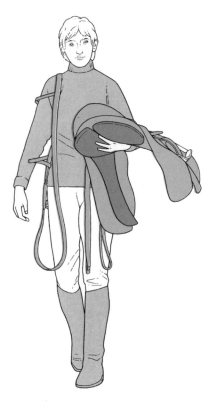

Above: Carry the bridle with the headpiece and reins over your left shoulder. Carry the saddle with the front arch in the crook of your left elbow. Alternatively, rest the cantle on your left hip and hold the front arch with your left hand. In either case, your right hand is free to open doors etc as necessary, and the cantle is protected from being scraped against walls or doors as you pass. A saddle is an expensive piece of equipment and should be treated with care. If properly looked after, it will last a lifetime.

The Quick-Release Knot

It is easier and safer to tie the horse up before you attempt to groom or saddle it. Occasionally a horse may be frightened and pull back or rear while it is tied up. There may be times when it is necessary to untie a horse in a hurry – in case of fire, for example. This is why the quick-release knot is always used. One pull on the loose end and the knot is undone.

In addition, the halter rope should be passed through a piece of string tied to the tethering ring. Then, if the horse should rear, the string will snap and the horse will not damage itself.

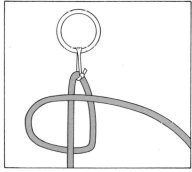

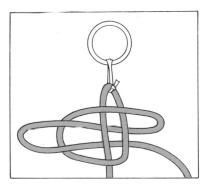

The horse should have been groomed thoroughly by the stable staff, but it may need tidying up. Use the dandy brush to remove any dried mud from the lower legs which may have gathered in a previous ride. Use firm flicking strokes. Slide your hand down the horse's quarters before you brush the lower legs. Brush the saddle patch thoroughly, and behind the front legs, where the girth lies. Any dirt or grit here will irritate the skin once the saddle is in position. Make sure there is no straw in the mane and tail and that the horse looks generally tidy. Lastly, pick out the feet, and then the horse is ready.

Putting on the Saddle

It is customary to put the saddle on first, before the bridle, so that the horse's back has time to 'warm up' before the rider mounts. The stirrups should be run up the leathers. The girth tabs should be done up on the offside only. If a fitted numnah is used, the straps or loops should be done up round the girth tabs. Fold the girth out of the way over the top of the saddle.

If you are using a martingale, put this on first, doing up the buckle on the nearside. Make sure the numnah is pulled up into the saddle arch, and place the saddle and numnah well forward of the withers. Slide them back into position, just behind the shoulder. This ensures that the hair under the saddle is lying flat.

Check that all is smooth under the saddle flap. Now go round the front of the horse and check the other side. Make sure the girth is not twisted. Stand at the nearside shoulder (out of kicking range) and reach under the horse's belly for the girth. Slip it through the martingale loop, and buckle it up firmly. You should still be able to slide your hand between the girth and the horse's side. The girth should not pinch the skin, which should lie smooth behind the horse's elbows.

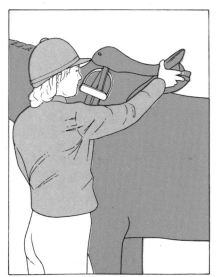

1. Put the saddle down lightly on the horse's back, well forward of the withers. The saddle can then slide back in the direction of the hair growth, so that all is smooth under the saddle.

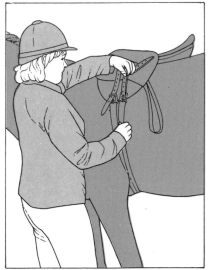

2. When you do up the buckles on the girth, make sure there are at least two more holes before the ends of the girth tabs. If not the girth is too short. The buckles should never lie directly against the horse's sides.

Putting on the Bridle

Make sure the bridle has been adjusted to fit your horse, and that the buckles of the throatlash and noseband are undone. You will obviously have to take off the headcollar before you can put on the bridle. Undo the lead rope and slip the reins over the horse's head. Now, when you take off the headcollar, you will have at least some control of the horse. The easiest way, I think, to put on the bridle is this. Stand close to the horse's head. Hold the bridle by the cheekpieces in your right hand, just in front of the horse's face. The bit should rest on the thumb and forefinger of your left hand. With your left forefinger, feel between the horse's lips at the side, where there are no teeth (the bars of the mouth). This makes the horse open its mouth. Slip in the bit, gently pulling up the cheekpieces. Use both hands to ease the headpiece over the horse's ears. Smooth out the mane and forelock. Do up the throatlash so you can get your hand between it and the horse's head. Do up a cavesson noseband inside the cheekpieces. Make sure you can get two fingers between the noseband and the front of the face. Now stand in front to check that everything is quite straight.

1. Some horse's object to being handled about the head. Approach an unknown horse with caution. Find the bars of the mouth (where there are no teeth) by slipping in your fingers behind the corners of the mouth.

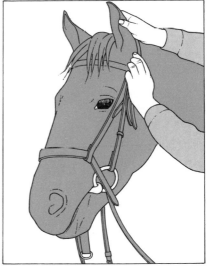

2. Slip the headpiece gently over the ears. Pull the forelock through so it lies on top of the browband. Make sure the browband has not ridden up so that it pinches the base of the ears, causing irritation.

Picking out the Horse's Feet

There is an old but accurate saying in riding circles – 'No foot, no horse'. In other words, if the horse's feet are not strong and healthy, you can forget the rest of the animal.

Working horses are prone to damage to the feet and lower legs which causes lameness. Care of the feet includes cleaning out the underside of the hoof regularly, using a hoofpick. This removes compacted muck and small stones and debris which often get wedged between the shoe and the frog. If these are left undisturbed disease may attack the foot, and stones can bruise or even pierce the sole once the weight of the rider is in the saddle.

When the foot is on the ground you can see the wall of the hoof. This grows down from the coronet continuously. In the wild, the wall is constantly worn away. When a horse has to work on roads and other hard surfaces the wall is worn away so quickly that it has to be protected by an iron shoe. At regular intervals depending on the shoe's wear and the rate of growth of the wall, the farrier removes the old shoes, trims the feet and reshoes the horse. The wall is insensitive so that the shoeing nails can be driven into it without damage to the horse. The circle of clenches – the ends of the nails – are hammered down flat against the wall of the food, about 2.5 cm (1 in) or so from the shoe.

The underside of the foot consists of the horny frog and the sole which you will be able to see when you pick up the foot. The 'V' shaped frog is sensitive so be careful when prodding round it with your hoofpick.

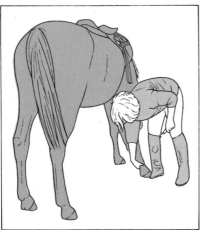

To pick up the foreleg, pat the horse's shoulder. Run your hand down the back of the leg. Squeeze the fetlock and say 'hup' as you lift the foot.

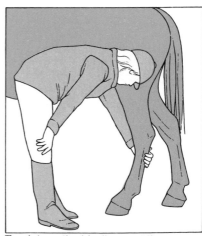

To pick up the hindleg, pat the quarters. Run your hand firmly down the back of the leg as far as the hock, then change to the inside of the leg.

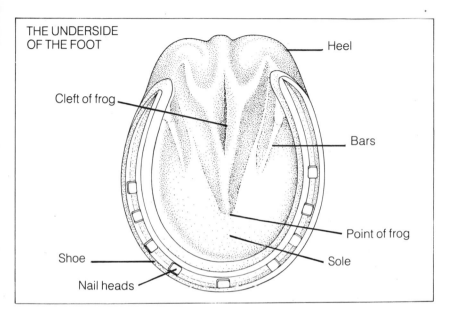

THE UNDERSIDE OF THE FOOT

Heel

Cleft of frog

Bars

Point of frog

Shoe

Sole

Nail heads

Above: The main structure you will notice on the underside of the foot is the frog. This helps give the horse grip, acts as a shock absorber and, incidentally, helps pump the blood back up the legs. The sole of the foot is concave which also assists the horse to grip. The sole is also thinner than the wall and more liable to damage. This shoe is slightly concave and fullered. i.e. a groove runs along its length for extra grip.

Right: When picking out the foot, work from the heel to the toe. Use your inside hand to hold the foot, and the outside hand to wield the pick. Hold the foot so that your hand is clear of the clenches – if the horse suddenly pulls its foot back, you could end up with some nasty scratches.

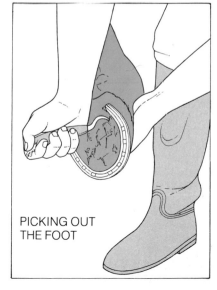

PICKING OUT THE FOOT

Returning Home

Near its home territory, a horse seems to know when the route turns towards the stable, almost before the rider. Its pace is likely to accelerate, so be prepared to steady it. In any case, if you are riding in a group and you want to overtake another rider, it is usual to call out a warning of your intentions, especially if you are overtaking at speed. Horses are herd animals, and their natural instinct is to keep together. If one animal in the group speeds up, the others will tend to follow suit.

You should aim to arrive back in the stable yard with your horse dry and pleasantly warm. This means that any fast work should be completed early enough in the ride for the horse to cool down, and any sweat to have dried. A hot sweaty horse cannot be put straight back in its loose box or it is likely to catch a chill. If a member of the stable staff has to spend half an hour leading your horse round in circles while it cools down, you will not endear yourself to them.

Once you have dismounted, run the stirrup irons up the leathers, loosen the girth and take the reins over the head, before leading the horse into its box. Wait for a few minutes before unsaddling to allow the horse's back to cool down.

To remove the bridle, put the reins back over the horse's head. Unbuckle the throatlash and noseband and then slip the headpiece over the ears. Have your left hand ready to take the bit as it slips out of the horse's mouth. Do not let it bang against the horse's teeth, as this can lead to the horse becoming

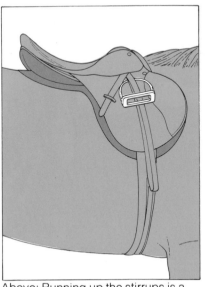

Above: Running up the stirrups is a safety precaution. It stops the irons banging against the horse's sides, or catching on doors and gates as you lead the horse through. When the stirrups are run up, assume that the girth is loose.

touchy about being bridled. Leave the reins over the head while you put on the headcollar, and then remove the reins before tying the horse up. To unsaddle, simply undo the girth on the nearside, and slide the saddle backwards and off the horse's back. It is customary to rub the saddle patch to restore circulation. Any sweat marks and dried mud should be brushed off straight away. (Leave wet mud to dry.)

A word of caution – never leave a horse, saddled and bridled, loose in its box after a ride. It is very likely to

get down and roll, seriously damaging the saddle. At best it will probably stand on the reins and break them!

In winter, working horses are usually clipped. This allows them to undertake fast work without sweating and losing condition under their natural thick winter coats. Clipped horses need rugs to keep them warm when they are not working, and these should be replaced as soon as the saddle and bridle have been removed.

In summer, your horse may be turned out into a field. As with most things equine, there is a right way and a wrong way to do this! Do not just walk into the field and slip off the headcollar. Most horses are delighted to go out for a rest, and may kick or buck as they rush off to greet their

Above: A horse is often quite excited when it is turned out in its field, so shut the gate before removing the headcollar. It often enjoys a good roll in the dust, undoing all your careful grooming!

companions. You cannot blame your horse if you happen to be in range. For safety's sake, go into the field, shut the gate, turn the horse round so its head is towards the gate, and then slip off the headcollar, giving the horse a quiet pat.

Rules and regulations seem to govern almost everything to do with horses. Riding is a long-established sport and over the years routines have become set. This can be irritating for the newcomer, but there is usually a sensible reason behind any given procedure.

The First Jumping Lesson

Walking over Poles

Your first jump is quite likely to be over a fallen log or small ditch, out on a ride. Your horse will probably pop over it quite happily with no help from you.

In the school, more formal lessons usually begin with walking and trotting calmly over poles spaced about 1.40 m (4ft 6in) apart. In an active trot, you should be able to feel the horse's back 'rounding'.

Above: As the horse negotiates poles or cavaletti, it stretches out its head and neck. Let your hands go forwards slightly on either side of the horse's neck, to allow for this movement. Do not throw the reins at the horse, letting them fall into loops. Maintain a light, even contact. At the end of the line of poles, sometimes turn right, sometimes left so that the horse does not anticipate your intentions.

Trotting over Poles

The next stage is to trot over a cavaletti placed about 2.75 m (9ft) from the last pole. Steer straight down the middle of the line of poles, look up and ahead, 'give' with your hands, and keep your legs close to the horse's sides.

As the jumps become a little more ambitious, you will have to modify your position to remain in balance with the horse. Shorten your stirrups by a hole or two. As you approach the jump, your weight should be slightly forward, taken on your thighs and knees and down into your heels, but keep your seat in contact with the saddle. Your knees and ankles should be flexible and ready to act as shock absorbers. As you pop over the jump, take your weight out of the saddle and fold forwards from the hips with back flat and head up. Look in the direction you want to go, not down at the jump. Practise the 'approach' and 'fold' position in trot and canter before

you try them out over cavaletti. There is no need to exaggerate them over small jumps.

Your early jumping practice will be chiefly in trot. The horse has to make more effort to jump out of trot so that you really get the feeling of popping over a good-sized jump, but at controllable speeds. Your horse is less likely to refuse, and you are less likely to be 'left behind' while your balance is still uncertain.

All this is good groundwork for the larger jumps to come.

Below: In the early stages, you may get 'left behind' as you go over the jump, and accidentally jab the horse in the mouth by pulling on the reins. Practising without reins prevents this from happening. It also develops the rider's confidence, and improves balance and position. Tie a knot in the reins and, as you approach the jump, drop the reins, fold your arms and use your legs to steer.

Jumping with Knotted Reins

Riding a Course

Once you can negotiate trotting poles with confidence, and pop over cavaletti, the next step is to trot over single jumps. At this stage, the jumps are probably about 60 cm high and 60 cm wide (2ft × 2ft). The width of the jump makes the horse use itself more athletically – important once the jumps get larger.

Although the jumps are small, you should still *ride* your horse. Keep your legs close to the horse's sides, and squeeze firmly if you feel any hesitation as you approach the jump. If the horse loses its forward impulsion, it will jump awkwardly and possibly unbalance you. As you circle in and out of the practice jumps, keep the trot even and active. Make your turns smooth. Don't suddenly point your horse at a jump, give it time to have a look. The horse and rider should take these little jumps completely in their stride.

Your first jump in canter will seem surprisingly smooth and easy after your trotting practice. Do not charge at the first jump you see. Plan a sequence of two or three jumps, including a change of direction. Trot into the first one, canter on, turn and pop over the next two. Come gently back into trot, then walk and give the horse a pat.

Two jumps, each about 60 cm (2ft) high, placed nearly seven metres (23ft) apart, make a simple double. Trot into the first part of the double, aiming to land in canter. You will have one non-jumping canter stride before the horse takes off again over the second part. Negotiating small doubles forces you to think ahead –

you cannot just collapse with relief once you are over the first part.

Riding a row of jumps in a straight line is not usually helpful, since it encourages the horse to rush. Six or seven simple jumps laid out in an enclosed space can provide a number of different routes, with plenty of changes of direction. The jumps should, ideally, be arranged so that you can take them from both directions. Newcomers to jumping sometimes find it difficult to remember the order in which they have to jump the fences. When your instructor suggests a course, try to think of the overall shape, rather than individual jumps.

When it is your turn to jump, trot a couple of active circles before you begin the course. If your horse has been standing quietly waiting its turn, this will give it a few moments to wake up and apply its mind to the work in hand. A horse is always likely to 'nap' towards other horses. Be prepared to ride positively as you pass the group, or you may be surprised by a run-out.

A good teacher will not make her students jump the same jumps or course over and over again. Horses (and riders!) quickly become stale and will start to make mistakes or misbehave. If the horse has completed the work successfully, it should be rewarded by a pat and by moving on to something new.

Right: A typical beginner's course might be laid out in a figure of eight. This ensures smooth, gentle turns to left and right, and a logical 'flow'. Approach each jump at right angles.

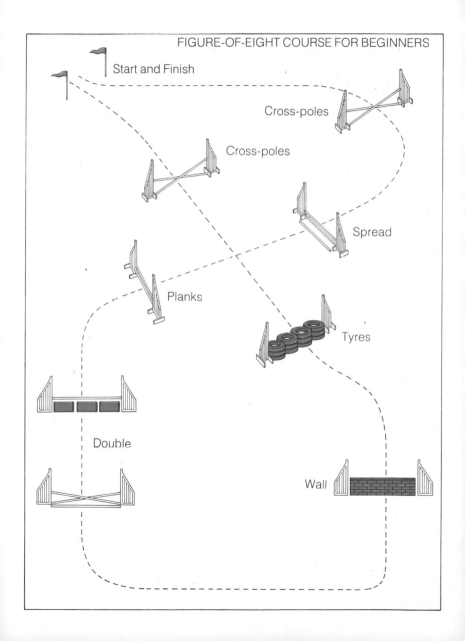

FIGURE-OF-EIGHT COURSE FOR BEGINNERS

Start and Finish

Cross-poles

Cross-poles

Spread

Planks

Tyres

Double

Wall

Beginner's Problems

A rider should not attempt to learn to jump until he is confident on the flat, and has a firm, independent seat. Your instructor should be able to advise you when you are ready.

When a horse is learning to jump, it is important that the rider is experienced. The reverse is also true.

A novice rider should always have his first jumping lessons on a horse that knows its job, and will, for the most part, 'take the rider round.' This gives the rider a chance to find out what it feels like to go over a jump before he has to deal with any problems.

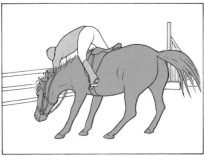

1. *My horse refuses.*
A horse will refuse if it is 'overfaced', i.e. presented with a fence which is too big. This is unlikely at this stage of your riding career. It is more often the case that the rider lacks confidence, and is not riding positively. If you tense up as you approach the jump your horse will sense it and refuse.

2. *My horse runs out.*
Again, if the horse is reasonably experienced, the likely reason is lack of rider confidence. Make sure you approach the jump *straight*, at a steady, active pace, with a proper contact on the reins, and squeeze firmly with your legs during the final few strides.

3. *My horse rushes at the jumps.*
A young excitable horse may rush at a jump in its eagerness to get to the other side. It may jump 'flat', not rounding its back, and knock the jump down, however small. Or, at the last minute, it may stop.

Trot evenly round the practice jumps until you feel that the horse is calm and 'listening' to you. Make a short approach in trot, give actively with your hands (but don't 'drop' the horse) and be ready to use your legs to prevent a stop.

4. *My horse turns sideways.*
This is a similar problem to the horse that rushes its fences. As the horse approaches the fence, it twists its body first one way, then the other, and usually dives at the fence at the last minute. It can be very unnerving for the rider. The answer again is to calm the horse by trotting smooth circles in and out of the jumps. Circle in front of your next jump and when you feel the horse is ready, turn it in to the jump. Don't forget leg yielding exercises. They can be used very effectively to control the horse's quarters, if these tend to swing sideways during the final approach.

Circling in Front of a Jump
This is a helpful exercise in a number of situations. Circling in trot will calm an excitable horse which is rushing its fences. It will also give you an opportunity to get the attention of a lazy horse. Make your circles fairly large. Give yourself plenty of room so that you make it quite clear to the horse in advance when you want it to continue on the circle, and when you want it to pop over the jump. Aids must be positive or you may, unintentionally, invite a refusal.

5. *My horse always seems to knock the jump down.*
While the jumps are still small, this is rarely because the horse has not got the energy to jump clear. Check your own position. Are you staying in balance with the horse, not jabbing its mouth, nor landing with a thump on its back after the jump? Any of these is enough to make the horse drop its hind legs into the jump. Otherwise, the problem is probably lack of impulsion. Make sure you have a proper rein contact. The horse must respond immediately to your leg aids before you turn in towards a jump, or you are asking for trouble.

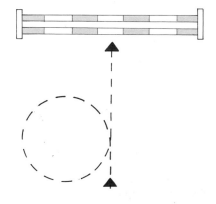

Entering a Horse Show

The advantages of entering a horse show are that it gives you a standard to aim for and measure your progress by. It is easier if you own your horse, but not impossible otherwise. Many riding establishments organise their own horseshows, including jumping competitions, and regular clients are usually encouraged to participate. If you live in a rural or semi-rural area, you may find small shows close enough to reach on horseback – obviating the need to hire and drive horseboxes or trailers.

Go along to one or two shows, with or without your horse, but without actually competing. You will get an idea of the standard required, and your horse will get used to being in close proximity with others. Take the advice of your instructor on local jumping competitions available. Bear in mind that small 'unaffiliated' shows will be less intimidating but can, sometimes, be less well organised than the larger shows which are affiliated to the British Show Jumping Association. To enter

an affiliated show, you must join the BSJA, and the smallest class for adults ranges in height from one metre to 1.06 m (3ft 3in to 3ft 6in) in the first round. Details of local shows are usually available at your riding school, or in the local press.

If you do not want to enter the show jumping arena, consider a novice hunter trial. The fastest clear round of a simple cross-country course wins. Dressage with jumping competitions are growing in popularity, and are excellent experience.

Below: It makes life much easier if you have an assistant to help. Leave time for a warm-up before you jump your round. This should, of course, begin with quiet flat work, building up to popping over the practice jump in the collecting ring. Do not jump it time and time again, and do not set it any higher than the competition jumps. It is always more difficult to tackle strange jumps in front of a crowd of people, so do not be too ambitious and enter too advanced a class at your first show.

PART 2 EQUESTRIAN SPORTS

The last ten years have seen a huge growth in the popularity of riding competitions as spectator sport. At the top of the list comes show jumping. Television was not slow to see the potential in its easy-to-follow rules, its big money prizes and the tension, building to a climax in the final rounds ridden against the clock. With wide television coverage has come the emergence of 'personalities', riders like Harvey Smith and family, David Broome and the Edgars.

Three-day-eventing is also growing in popularity, especially the cross-country element of the competition. We are fortunate in Britain to host the world's premier three-day event on the Duke of Beaufort's estate at Badminton. Quite apart from the millions who watch the television coverage, 250,000 people go in person to see the world's top event riders compete – more than attend any other sporting event, except perhaps Derby Day!

Long distance riding has a large following in the USA and Australia and is becoming more common in Europe. Its appeal is that it relies more on skill and horsemanship than on having a valuable thoroughbred.

Once you have gained a reasonable level of riding competence yourself, you will be able to appreciate the experts more fully.

Right: Graham Fletcher, riding Cool Customer, pushes on towards a water jump. To be sure of clearing a water jump the horse must stretch out, while still gaining good height, if it is not to drop a foot in the water.

Dressage

What is Dressage?

In terms of popular interest, dressage is the poor relation of equestrian sports. To the uninitiated, it is not as spectacular as a jumping competition. There is no absolute standard since the placings of competitors depend on the subjective judgement of one or two individuals.

Many riders, too, are put off dressage because of its foreign name and the general feeling that it consists of an obscure and specialised system of communication.

In fact, the word dressage comes from the French 'dresser', to train. For top show jumpers and eventers, dressage training is an essential preliminary to their jumping work. Only through dressage, can the horse build up the flexibility and muscular control needed to cope with the demanding athletic effort of international competition.

Even the average riding horse can be made more obedient, more comfortable and an altogether better ride by simple dressage training.

Dressage consists of an ordered series of gymnastic movements which the horse performs in order to improve its natural outline and paces, and to become more supple and obedient. A horse in a field, or in the early stages of training, moves with a long, low outline. Its head and neck are carried low and stretched out. With dressage training over many months, the horse is gradually encouraged to shorten that outline and to become more 'collected'. The head and neck are raised, the back is rounded and the quarters are used more actively so that they are brought further under the horse's body. The centre of gravity of the horse moves backwards. When a horse can show some 'collection', it can respond more quickly to the rider's aids, stopping, starting and turning, accelerating and decelerating instantly.

A highly trained dressage horse corresponds to a human gymnast. Like a gymnast, expertise is only achieved after years of training.

Dressage Competitions

The competing riders perform the same set series of movements which make up a dressage test. The test is divided into sections, each containing movements and transitions. Each section is marked out of 10 by one, two or three judges, depending on the level of the competition. At the end of the test, marks out of 10 are also awarded for general impression; obedience and calmness; paces and impulsion; position and seat of the rider and correct application of the aids.

There are dressage tests for every standard, starting with the Preliminary tests, followed by Novice, Elementary, Medium, and

Top right: An example of a dressage test sheet of the Novice standard. The competitor has to learn the test so that he can perform it from memory.

Bottom right: Britain's most successful competitive dressage rider is Jennie Lorriston-Clarke, here seen riding Kadett. She came third in the 1978 World Championships.

Price — 5p

THE BRITISH HORSE SOCIETY'S
DRESSAGE TEST
NUMBER 17
(Novice standard) 1980

			Max. Marks
1.	A	Enter at working trot	
	X	Halt. Salute. Proceed at working trot	10
	C	Track left	10
2.	E	Circle left 20m. diameter	10
3.	K	Half circle left 10m. diameter returning to the track at H	10
4.	B	Circle right 20m. diameter	10
5.	F	Half circle right 10m. diameter returning to the track at M	10
6.	C	Working trot (rising)	
	HXF	Change rein and show some lengthened strides (rising)	10
	F	Working trot (sitting)	
7.	KXM	Change rein and show some lengthened strides (rising)	10
	M	Working trot (sitting)	
8.	C	Medium walk	
	HBK	Free walk on a long rein	10
	K	Medium walk	
9.	A	Working trot	10
	F	Working canter left	10
10.	B	Circle left 20m. diameter	10
11.	HXF	Change rein and stroke the horse's neck	10
	F	Working trot	
12.	K	Working canter right	10
	E	Circle right 20m. diameter	
13.	MXK	Change rein and stroke the horse's neck	10
	K	Working trot	
14.	A	Down centre line	10
	G	Halt. Immobility. Salute	
		Leave arena at walk on a long rein at A	
15.		General impression, obedience and calmness	10
16.		Paces and impulsion	10
17.		Position and seat of the rider and correct application of the aids.	10
		TOTAL	**170**

Advanced. Higher still are the tests used in international competitions, the Prix St George, Intermediaire I, Intermediaire II, Grand Prix and Grand Prix Special.

Dressage has a stronger tradition in continental Europe than in Britain. This is perhaps because the heavier continental horse is better suited temperamentally to dressage than the hot-blooded English Thoroughbred. At any international competition it is usually the Germans who dominate. In Britain, however, pure dressage is finding a growing band of supporters, and more young riders are achieving the higher standards necessary to compete internationally. Our most successful dressage rider is Jennie Lorriston-Clarke who was bronze medallist in the 1978 World Championships, on her Advanced horse, Dutch Courage.

If you are interested in competing in dressage competitions at whatever level, join the local branch of the affiliated Riding Club. This usually has a band of dressage enthusiasts, who will help and advise you. To compete in affiliated National Dressage, or Dressage with Jumping Competitions, you must be a member of the Dressage Group of the British Horse Society.

Dressage to Music

Since one of the requirements of a good dressage test is regular rhythm, it is not surprising that dressage can be performed very successfully to music. The music has to be planned to fit the individual horse's paces, including transitions, as well as the test but, sensitively put together, dressage with music can be very impressive. In addition, exponents say that the horse relaxes and can even learn to slow or quicken to fit the rhythm of the music. Dressage with music competitions are now being held, which include marks for artistic impression, and they are proving popular.

The collected paces are the most difficult to perform. In the collected trot (above left), the outline is rounded and shortened. The horse takes short but very active steps. In the extended trot (above right), the outline is slightly longer. The horse's steps are lower and cover more ground, but they must not be faster. Between the collected and extended trots there is the working trot, used for Preliminary and Novice work.

Above: The pirouette can be performed at walk or canter. The horse makes a small circle, the forehand moving round the hind quarters.

Left: The half pass is another movement on two tracks. The horse moves diagonally, its body parallel with the long side of the arena.

Above: In dressage training, much effort goes into making the horse more supple along its length. When the horse is on a circle, its spine should bend smoothly, following the direction of the curve. It is important that on a straight line, the horse should be 'straight', with its hind legs following in the tracks of the forelegs. This is more difficult than it sounds, as many horses tend to swing their quarters out to the side.

Show Jumping

The Beginnings

The father of modern show jumping is said to be the Italian, Captain Frederico Caprilli. He developed the jumping style used today, whereby the rider stays in balance with the horse by shifting his weight forward when the horse takes off. It obviously enables the horse to jump with maximum height and accuracy if the rider is balanced and does not hinder the horse by, for example, landing heavily on its back in the middle of a jump.

Show jumping competitions were first held at agricultural shows at the end of the nineteenth century. The judges had a difficult job, since marks were awarded for riding style, and more faults were earned if the horse knocked down the jump with its forelegs than with its hindlegs.

Right: Harvey Smith is one of the most ebullient characters on the showjumping scene and in his long career he has won practically every major competition in Britain. Here he is seen with Salvador, a brilliant German horse, who was a top prize winner in his day.

How the Sport is Organised

The BSJA (British Show Jumping Association) was founded in 1923. The major shows are affiliated to the BSJA, and are run according to its rules. Most people, however, get their first show jumping experience at small, non-affiliated shows held in the summer all over the country. They have classes for all sizes and standards, from 'minimus' upwards.

Grading

Under BSJA rules, horses are graded according to the prize money they have won: Grade C, novice (up to £300); Grade B, intermediate (£300–£800); Grade A, advanced (£800 plus).

Note that it is the horse, not the rider, which is graded. At many affiliated shows, spectators have the opportunity of watching the top stars put their new young horses through their paces.

The BSJA publishes a Year Book giving information about the grading system, and the rules governing types of competition. To compete at affiliated shows, you must be a BSJA member.

Course Building

Good course building for show jumping is vital. The track must be suitable for the level of competition – too easy and the competition will over-run, too hard and a horse and rider could be injured. The height is only one consideration. More important are the types of jumps, the distances between them, the related distances in combinations and direction changes in jump-offs.

Show Jumping as Big Business

To stay at the necessary high standard, most top show jumpers are full-time professionals. The costs involved are enormous. A good, young horse, unbroken and totally untried as a jumper, might cost £5,000–£10,000. After years of training it might climb through the grades to reach international level, when it would be worth £100,000 or more, but very few horses do make the grade. Even though the horse may have the talent, veterinary problems could put an end to its career. A horse is broken in at four years, but is still considered young for advanced classes at seven or eight. Landing after a jump causes jarring to the forelegs, and this can build into serious trouble over the years. Not surprisingly, riders nurse their top horses carefully, saving them for the most prestigious shows.

In addition, the running costs are estimated at £3,000–£4,000 per year to keep a show jumper. Most top riders have a string, including two or three good horses and a number of up-and-coming youngsters in training.

Even the prize money from the big shows is not enough to support a team. With increased media coverage, however, commercial sponsorship was introduced and now many teams are financed in this way.

Right: A combination jump consists of two or three parts. They usually allow one or two non-jumping strides between parts, or require the horse to 'bounce' in and out. The horse must adjust its take-off accordingly.

Treble consisting of wall, followed by a spread, followed by parallel bars.

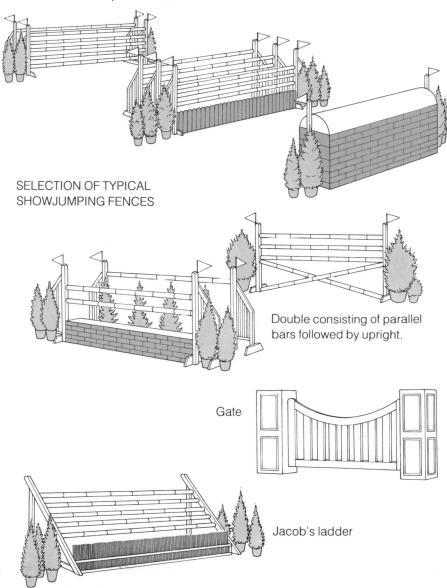

SELECTION OF TYPICAL
SHOWJUMPING FENCES

Double consisting of parallel bars followed by upright.

Gate

Jacob's ladder

Eventing

Eventing is the ultimate test of all-round performance in horse and rider. It derives from a military competition – in fact years ago, it was known as 'the military'. The horse must be fast and bold across country, supremely fit, yet calm enough to perform a good dressage test.

A three-day event is divided into sections and marked on a penalty basis. A multiplying factor is used to determine the relative importance of each section so that the middle test, the speed, endurance and cross-country, has the strongest influence.

Dressage Test
On the first day, competitors perform their dressage test, which in three-day eventing can be up to Medium standard. The main difficulty is that event horses have to be jumping out of their skins with fitness to perform in the cross-country the next day. So a cool, calm dressage performance is no easy feat!

Speed and Endurance
On the second day, the speed and endurance test takes place. There is an optimum time allowed, and competitors do not gain extra marks for coming home faster than this. *Phase A* consists of three or four miles of roads and tracks, taken at a steady trot. *Phase B* is a steeplechase course, which usually has to be taken at a racing gallop to avoid accumulating time penalties. *Phase C* follows straight away with more roads and tracks. There follows a break of a few minutes before the cross-country course begins. This allows time for the horse to have a few minutes breather, for tack to be checked over and the horse washed down.

Show Jumping
On the final morning, a veterinary inspection takes place, to be followed by a relatively simple show-jumping course. The competitors have to change from the galloping style of the cross-country, and jump more carefully. The main aim of this test is to show that the horse is supple and obedient, despite the exertions of the previous day.

Badminton and Burghley are at the top of the eventing scale. Below these are many two-day and one-day events. To compete in BHS affiliated events, riders must be members of the BHS Horse Trials group. Their horses earn points as they compete, and are graded as follows: Grade III, novice (less than 21 points); Grade II, intermediate (21–60 points); Grade I, advanced (61 or more points).

Events take place in spring and summer. The more popular ones are often over-subscribed so that a balloting system has to be used to determine entries.

The Cross-Country Section
Competitors are counted down to the start, at intervals of a few min-

Right: The Badminton Three-Day Event course stays largely the same, except that it is reversed in alternate years. Thus certain cross-country jumps have to be omitted, and new jumps are occasionally incorporated.

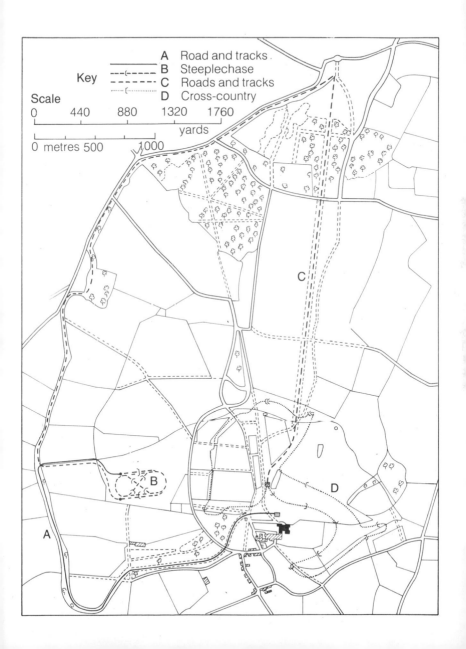

Key

A   Road and tracks
B   Steeplechase
C   Roads and tracks
D   Cross-country

Scale

| 0 | 440 | 880 | 1320 | 1760 |

yards

0 metres 500   1000

utes. This means that there are several competitors on the course at the same. time, the fastest competitor having right of way.

Cross-country obstacles are fixed – that is they cannot be knocked down should a horse hit them. This makes them potentially more dangerous than show jumps since a mistake can lead to a serious fall of horse or rider. The early jumps on the course are usually inviting and straight-forward. Later come the more difficult combination, drop and water jumps. There are usually alternative routes through, but to be in the money, a rider usually has to take the time-saving but trickiest route. A fall of horse or rider, refusals or taking the wrong course all incur penalties which are added to any time faults.

At the end of this most taxing part of the competition, the horses are carefully checked for bruises, cuts or any other damage. Early treatment may help prevent serious trouble later, and prepares the horse for the veterinary inspection on the following morning. This is a most nerve-wracking time for the rider since if his horse does not trot up sound before the vet, it will be disqualified.

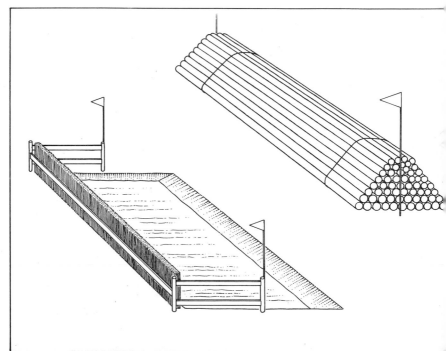

Below: Unlike brightly coloured show jumps, cross country obstacles are designed to look 'natural', using banks, walls, fallen trees, water or the occasional farmyard feature such as a hayrick or sheep pen. Course builders can use their imaginations to devise ingenious 'combination' jumps. The more confident rider can save valuable time by taking the shortest but most difficult route.

Because cross country jumps are fixed, they are not usually as wide or as high as the equivalent standard of show jump, but they are potentially more dangerous, and just as unnerving to the imaginative rider.

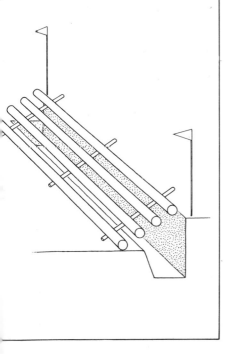

Above: Special Equipment for the Cross Country Phase
1. Safety helmet with 'silk' cover
2. Rider's number
3. Stop watch
4. Back support
5. Gloves
6. Tail bandage
7. Boots or bandages
8. Overreach boots on forelegs
9. Horse's number
10. Additional sircingle over saddle
11. Grease on front of legs to help the horse slide over obstacles.

Hunting

Hunting has played a very important part in Britain's riding tradition. Riding in company for miles across country, and jumping a variety of natural obstacles, is a thrilling experience for both horse and rider. For most people who go hunting, it is this experience that appeals, not the killing of the fox. Throughout the winter, some 200 foxhunting packs meet regularly, two or three days a week. There are also drag hunts, when hounds follow a scent laid by 'dragging' a trail across country.

Each hunt is governed by the rules of the MFHA (Master of Foxhounds Association), and towards the end of the season, holds a point-to-point race meeting. To qualify to race, a horse must have hunted

regularly in that season, so the point-to-point provides racing for the relative amateur.

Hunting offers a unique opportunity for fast riding across unprepared countryside. This background helps explain why Britain does so well in show jumping and eventing, world-wide. Horses which have learned to look after themselves in the hunting field have often proved to be outstanding competition horses later.

Below: Mr Goschen's foxhounds await instructions. A well trained pack is vital to preserve good relations in the countryside. The hounds (never called 'dogs') are as carefully bred for performance as race horses.

Long Distance Riding

This is a branch of equestrian sport which has a growing following. It combines the competitive spirit with superb horsmanship, yet without the dangers inherent in jumping. A good long distance horse is also unlikely to be an expensive thoroughbred, and so success in this sphere is brought within reach of the many horsemen and women who cannot afford to enter the show-jumping or eventing arenas.

The Competitions
Official competitions range from Pleasure Rides, to Trial Rides, Endurance Rides, One to Three day Rides and Ride and Tie (in which two riders take it in turn to ride and run with one horse). In the longest rides, 75 to 100 miles may be covered in one day over rough and hilly terrain. To take part in the top competitions, horses usually have to prove themselves by competing in certain qualifying rounds.

In long distance competitions, the welfare of the horse is very much to the forefront. Riders receive awards for completing the course within certain time limits and with the horse in good condition. Like human marathon running, there may only be one overall winner, but any competitor completing the course is usually more interested in his or her personal best times.

Along the route there are check points so that stages of the course are completed within certain optimum times. The condition of the horse, its pulse and respiration are checked, and if not up to the required standard, it has to be retired.

In the past, horses pushed over very long distances were known to collapse and die. Today they can cover 100 miles in 15 hours or so and come home fresh. This is largely due to our increased knowledge of how to prepare horses so that they are properly fit.

The Long Distance Horse
There is no one type of horse bred for endurance riding. Many kinds have proved successful in the hands of the right rider/trainer. In general, good distance horses tend to be smaller than jumpers, about 15 to 16 hands. Good stamina, sound legs and feet and comfortable paces are obviously essential.

Training
Building up fitness in any horse demands months of work, and is part of the horsemaster's art. It begins with gentle walking to toughen the legs. Long, slow trots up and down hill are introduced to increase stamina. Basic flat work develops the horse's natural balance and improves its paces. Feeding must be adjusted to suit the amount of work being done to keep the horse full of energy, not over-full. Perhaps as important as any of these is building up the rapport that exists in any successful partnership.

Right: In days past, it was thought to be dangerous to let horses drink during long rides and as a result the horses sometimes suffered. Today, they are encouraged to drink whenever possible, the rule now being that 'little and often' is best.

Useful Addresses

The British Horse Society
The British Equestrian Centre
Stoneleigh
Kenilworth
Warwickshire CV8 2LR
Tel: (0203) 52241

This is a national body which caters for the interests of riders and promotes the welfare of the horse. It can offer guidance on many aspects of riding, in both its competitive and leisure branches. It publishes a range of books and pamphlets on where to learn, how to ride, and the care and training of horses. It offers a widely-known series of tests on riding and stable management for Pony Club members, older riders, and students planning a career with horses. It also runs an inspection system. Riding establishments displaying a plaque, 'Approved by the BHS', have had their premises and horses inspected and usually offer better facilities than the basic level which can be licensed by local authorities.

To take part in the many BHS affiliated competitions, it is necessary to be a member of the BHS and the particular branch which applies to your sport. Contact the BHS for further information about:
Road safety
Bridleways
Riding holidays
Careers advice
Riding tests and exams
The Pony Club
The Affiliated Riding Club
Buying a horse or pony
Where to ride

Competitive riding
Horse Trials
Dressage
Horse Driving
Long Distance Riding
Show Jumping
It publishes books and pamphlets on the care and training of horses, and learning to ride.

The Association of British Riding Schools
Mrs J. Earl (Secretary)
44 Market Jew Street
Penzance
Cornwall
Tel: (0736) 69440

This is the professional organization for riding school proprietors. It has designed a graded series of tests, on riding skills and stable management, for the rider who is not necessarily a horse owner. It publishes its own *Handbook of Where to Ride*. Riding schools may only become members of the ABRS after their premises and teaching methods have been inspected. These schools usually provide better facilities than the basic level which may be licensed by the local authority.

Ponies of Britain
Mrs E. Merry (Secretary)
Ascot Race Course
Ascot
Berks SL5 7JN
Tel: (0990) 26925

This organization aims to promote the well-being of ponies and, in particular, the nine breeds of pony native to Britain. It disseminates information about the history of the breeds, caring for ponies, and advises on breeding. It holds a number of shows annually, when prime examples of the native breeds can be seen.

In parallel with this work, Ponies of Britain run an inspection scheme for trekking and riding holiday centres. Establishments which have won POB certificates should offer better facilities than the basic level which can be licensed. POB also supplies a booklet, *Approved Riding Holiday Centres* which has useful information on size, facilities offered, opening dates etc.

Riding Holidays

Many people have their first experience of riding on holiday. If you are planning a riding holiday for novice riders, consider what you want to get out of it. If you have never ridden before, hours in the saddle every day may be excruciating and put you off the sport completely. Some centres combine riding with another sport, offer films and lectures on different aspects of riding, or are situated close to places of interest to visit etc. These are well worth considering.

There are basically three types of riding holiday:

1 Trekking Good for beginners if daily treks are not too long. Consists of gentle rides at walk and trot in countryside often inaccessible by any other method. Return to base each night. Minimum instruction necessary is given.

2 Trail Riding For more experienced riders. Longer distances covered across country, usually staying at different lodgings or camping each night. Equipment may be carried on pack ponies, or taken on ahead by alternative transport.

3 Riding Centre If your main priority is to learn to ride, not just to enjoy the countryside, this is the best choice. Ideally a good riding holiday should offer periods of instruction, interspersed with hacking out in pleasant surroundings, and practical sessions of stable management. Lectures and films may also be offered. To get the best out of this kind of holiday, you need to be reasonably fit before you start.

Brief Bibliography

On riding and training horses.
The Manual of Horsemanship
Training the Young Pony
Both are Pony Club publications available from the BHS.
On Stable Management:
There are many to choose from. A good starting point is *Keeping a Pony at Grass*, a Pony Club Publication, available from the BHS.
On veterinary care:
Know Your Horse – A Guide to Selection and Care in Health and Disease by Lt Colonel W. S. Codrington, (J. A. Allen & Co).
The TV Vet Horse Book – Recognition and Treatment of Common Horse and Pony Ailments (Farming Press Ltd).

Index

Acknowledgements
The author would like to thank Stephanie Berridge of the
Applemore Equitation Centre, Hampshire, for sharing her own
particular brand of enthusiasm for horses; Peter Roberts, FBHS,
for his helpful observations on the text and the British
Horse Society for permission to reproduce the dressage test sheet
on page 75.